FOLKLORE
YORKSHIRE

KAI ROBERTS

The
History
Press

For Miss Kathryn Adelaide Wilson (of the Moors).

First published 2013

The History Press
The Mill, Brimscombe Port
Stroud, Gloucestershire, GL5 2QG
www.thehistorypress.co.uk

© Kai Roberts, 2013
The right of Kai Roberts to be identified as the Author
of this work has been asserted in accordance with the
Copyright, Designs and Patents Act 1988.

British Library Cataloguing in Publication Data.
A catalogue record for this book is available from the British Library.

ISBN 978 0 7524 8579 9

Typesetting and origination by The History Press
Printed in Great Britain

FOLKLORE
YORKSHIRE

CONTENTS

Acknowledgements

Thanks to John Billingsley, Dr David Clarke, Jonathan Dow, Anna O'Loughlin, Tania Poole, Matilda Richards, Andy Roberts, Helen Roberts, Phil Roper and John Warren.

INTRODUCTION

In the present day, two questions may naturally arise when a book such as this is encountered: what is 'folklore', and what value does it have? When the word was first coined by W.J. Thoms in 1846, the answers were relatively easy. Folklore was an attempt to record, systematise and preserve what had previously been referred to as 'popular antiquities' – the beliefs and practices of the 'folk'; a poorly educated and primarily rural class whose indigenous, insular culture was perceived as threatened by the rapid advance of industrialisation and urbanisation. Such people were typically regarded as quite separate from the refined, scholarly collectors, and, as the historian E.P. Thompson so scathingly put it, 'Folklore in England is largely a literary record of eighteenth- and nineteenth-century survivals, recorded by parsons and by genteel antiquarians regarding them across a gulf of class condescension.'

Today, with the advent of universal education, global communications, mass media and a mobile population, it is impossible to regard the 'folk' in such a detached, homogenous manner – if it was ever truly possible in the first place. We are all immersed in popular culture and we are all members of many social groups over the course of our lives; whether those groups be determined by generation, geography, ethnicity, occupation, religion, hobby or economic status. The boundaries are permeable, flexible and almost impossible to identify. As a result, the term 'folklore' increasingly looks anachronistic and yet somehow it survives; for no matter how nebulous the concept might be, it still identifies an area of knowledge worthy of study in its own right and too often overlooked by its close cousins, social history and ethnography.

The best definition of folklore we can find today comes from Jacqueline Simpson and Steve Roud: 'It includes whatever is voluntarily and informally communicated, created or done jointly by members of a group (of any size, age, or social and educational level) ... The essential criterion is the presence of a group whose joint sense of what is right and appropriate shapes the story, performance or custom – not the rules and teachings of any official body.' The value of studying such material lies not just in preserving it but in learning to recognise what counts as folklore, because often it provides a rare insight into the hidden assumptions and unrecognised priorities of the culture that spawned it; whilst historically, it offers a valuable alternative narrative to the 'authorised' or 'official' accounts supplied by the hegemonic interests in that society.

Of course, this book does not have quite such high ambitions. In the history of folklore studies, the county folklore collection has been something of an institution. In the early days of the discipline, they provided a great deal of the material with which folklorists subsequently worked and whilst they have slowly calcified into a product primarily marketed to tourists, they remain one of the primary sources of folkloric material available to a general readership. This work undoubtedly falls into the latter category, but whilst it does not aim for originality or innovation, it will hopefully do more than merely repeat material which has been printed in such collections a hundred times before without context or analysis. Folklore is something that once possessed meaning for those who lived with it and it should not be reduced to mere whimsy or entertainment.

An entrenched problem with county folklore collections, dating back to the very first examples, has been their failure to properly consider the environment in which it was typically transmitted and the significance it was afforded by those who communicated it. Either the original collector imposed his own beliefs on the material or failed to regard it as anything more than a novelty. As Gillian Bennett complains, 'For the most part, no great care was taken to make any sort of *sense* of these stories. They were simply "stories" and not *expected* to make sense: they were curiosities rather than realities. There was no attempt to put them in context either: we do not know when or why or how or to whom the legends were told ... Such accounts do not tell us what ... traditions meant to the informant: they only tell us what they meant to the collectors – which was *precisely nothing*.'

A common difficulty with such collections is that they were often rooted in the folkloric theory of the nineteenth century. Influenced by the reductive academic climate of the day, early folklorists took inspiration from the emerging theory of evolution and attempted to apply it their own material. The result was the hypothesis of 'survivals', which claimed that whilst human history and culture was often a progressive, dynamic process, some features remained relatively static: these remnants gradually lost their original function and significance to become 'folklore', preserved in debased form by the collective memory of a conservative rural working class. The early folklorists believed that by studying these relics, it was possible to reconstruct the religious belief of pre-Christian societies.

As a result of this assumption, English folklore studies developed an obsession with continuity. For something to be regarded as 'folklore', it was thought to have remained unchanged for countless centuries and be 'fixed' so that no further collection was necessary. The same old stories were reprinted again and again in folklore anthologies, under the mistaken impression that folklore never moved on; whilst commentaries on this material never considered the unique circumstances which might have produced an individual legend or custom, nor the needs they might have fulfilled. It is an error which has been repeated by county folklore collections down the ages, and although academic folklore studies have advanced considerably in the last fifty years, new ways of thinking about the subject have rarely filtered through to popular books on the subject.

The truth is, however, that even the most insular, rural populations were rarely as conservative as the early folklorists believed. New traditions often developed in response to changing populations and circumstances, and even the oldest surviving customs underwent constant revision over the centuries. Some continuity does exist, but it was a dynamic rather than a static process, and the emphasis needs to be placed on how and why such development occurs. Similarly, the turnover of some traditions is very rapid indeed and a great deal of what is popularly thought of as 'folklore' is merely the folklore of the nineteenth century, preserved by uncritical repetition in printed texts over the last 150 years. Much of this material has not been relevant since it was first collected and bears scant resemblance to the 'folklore' that circulates in modern society. Yet we are so immersed in the folklore of our own age, that often we do not even recognise it.

A truly twenty-first century 'Folklore of Yorkshire' would include such topics as ufology, conspiracy theories, urban legends, aliens, big cats, email rumours and more, but this is not that book. Such a project would probably take a lifetime of collection to compile and owing to the dynamic nature of the phenomena it dealt with, would be obsolete long before it was finished. This work can only ever be *A* Folklore of Yorkshire – no definitive article – and one that will primarily deal with historical material at that. But whilst it will repeat some familiar legends and hopefully bring one or two gleaned from obscure sources to a larger audience, its purpose is not just to repeat stories without any reference to their wider meaning. Instead, the material will be treated as the vehicle by which centuries of Yorkshire folk expressed their hopes, fears and beliefs in response to ever-changing and diverse circumstances – a dynamic, creative process which continues today.

Kai Roberts, 2013

ONE

WITCHES AND CUNNING FOLK

It is an incongruity often observed that the most acute phase of witch hysteria in England occurred not in the Middle Ages – commonly decried as the zenith of scientific ignorance and superstition – but in the first half of the seventeenth century, even as the first seeds of the Enlightenment were being sown. There is ample evidence to suggest that Yorkshire was as much embroiled in the witch craze as any other region, but whilst there were undoubtedly a number of associated executions in the county, there were no episodes as egregious as the Pendle Witch Trials which gripped neighbouring Lancashire in 1612, or 'Witchfinder General', Matthew Hopkins' reign of terror in East Anglia from 1644 to 1646.

Yorkshire's most famous witch-hunt occurred around Washburndale in 1621 and was amply documented by its instigator in the pamphlet 'A Discourse on Witchcraft as it was acted in the family of Mr. Edward Fairfax of Fewston in the County of York in the year 1621 AD'. Fairfax was an accomplished writer whose work was praised by future Poet Laureate John Dryden, but it seems that he possessed a misanthropic disposition which often brought him into conflict with his less educated neighbours after he inherited Newhall at Fewston (now submerged beneath Swinsty Reservoir) from his father in 1600. His contempt for them is clear throughout his work: 'Such a wild place,' he writes, 'Such rude people upon whose ignorance God have mercy!'

Doubtless the locals regarded Fairfax with similar disdain, and, by 1621, tensions erupted in accusations of witchcraft. Fairfax charged eight Fewston women with working enchantments on his three daughters, Ellen, Elizabeth and Ann: he claimed they had caused the girls to suffer from fits, trances, 'irrational behaviour' and, on one occasion, temporary blindness. Meanwhile, every minor misfortune the family suffered, Fairfax did not hesitate to attribute to witchcraft. For instance, when Elizabeth fell from an insecure haymow and injured herself, he perceived it to be the work of Bess Fletcher, who was watching the child at the time. His suspicions were only confirmed when Ann died of natural causes during infancy.

Fairfax also claimed to have evidence of the alleged witches' malefic intent. Supposedly an old widow named Margaret Thorpe had been seen casting images of his daughters into a stream; lamenting if they floated, but cheering if they sank. Perhaps most fancifully, he accused the women of abducting his daughters and forcing them to attend a Midsummer's Eve bonfire on the surrounding moors – a superstitious and possibly pagan survival which to Fairfax's Puritanical mind was identical with diabolism. However, to the credit of the local authorities – including Fewston's vicar, Henry Greaves – all such 'evidence' was dismissed as circumstantial or hearsay and Fairfax twice failed to have the women convicted at York Assizes. Following their release, the women held a great celebration in Timble Gill, over which Fairfax insisted the Devil himself had presided.

Contrary to popular belief, this is how most witch trials concluded. Although accusations of witchcraft were rife in the seventeenth century, only 30 per cent of those indicted were actually convicted. The spate of such allegations around that time was largely due to familiar social tensions heightened by the febrile religious atmosphere that followed the Reformation. As social historian Keith Thomas notes, whilst the Reformation had aimed to purge Christianity of superstitious practices, it actually heightened superstitious dread amongst the majority of the population. Protestantism emphasised the power of the Devil, yet by prohibiting the characteristically Catholic rite of exorcism, simultaneously removed the ordinary person's best defence against his work. As such, paranoia increased but it could only now be defused through the secular courts rather than harmless religious ritual.

The Reformation also brought about a change in attitude towards the poor. Whilst Catholicism had stressed the religious importance of almsgiving through the Middle Ages, Protestantism was much more individualistic and exalted the idea of self-reliance. This exacerbated social conflict, increasing ill-feeling on both sides of the divide: the poor resented the new mercantile class for their reluctance to give alms, whilst the merchants resented the poor for begging for them. The potential consequence of this dynamic can be seen in the Heptonstall witch trial of 1646. In the week before Michaelmas, Elizabeth Crossley had been refused alms at the house of Henry Cockroft and left muttering imprecations. Thus, when Cockroft's infant son began to suffer fits two nights later, from which he eventually died, the finger of blame was pointed straight at Crossley.

But whilst Elizabeth Crossley was probably just an innocent beggar with a temper, the issue was compounded by the fact that some outsiders who were otherwise ostracised by the community exploited their reputation for witchcraft in order to gain some modicum of deference from their neighbours. Their perceived

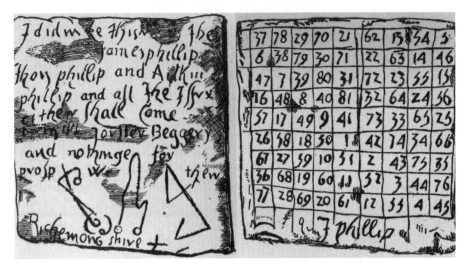

Gatherley Moor Witch Tables.

power was the art of 'maleficium' – causing harm to people or property through the use of sorcery. It was essentially 'black magic', as opposed to the 'white magic' practiced by 'wise' men and women, whose skills were primarily directed towards healing, finding lost items and defence against maleficium. Yet when the charms of such people failed – for instance, if a potion they had administered to cure an illness was coincidentally followed by the death of the patient – it was easy for such people to be accused of maleficium themselves.

Furthermore, there is evidence to suggest that rare individuals may have offered malefic services. In the nineteenth century, two lead tablets dated to 1575 were found buried in a tumulus on Gatherley Moor. They were described as 'quadrangular with several planetary marks, rude scratches and an inscription on one side; and on the other are figures set in arithmetical proportion from 1 to 81 and so disposed in parallel and equal ranks, that the sum of each row, as well diagonally and horizontally as perpendicularly is equal to 369.' The inscription states that these 'witch tables' were spells to cause the Philips family to flee Richmondshire or forever fail to prosper there and as they were signed by John Philips, this unambiguous act of maleficium must have arisen from a family dispute, possibly over the terms of a will.

By the end of the seventeenth century, belief in witchcraft was dying out amongst the educated classes. The last executions for the 'crime' occurred in Exeter in 1682 and its definition was revised by the 1735 Witchcraft Act, so that the offence became one of fraud rather than harmful intent. In Yorkshire, the trend was no different: even evangelically religious sources were growing sceptical about such accusations and in May 1683, the radical nonconformist preacher, Reverend Oliver Heywood, scathingly dismissed the concerns of a member of his Calderdale congregation who feared her twelve-year-old son had been bewitched. Yet despite the increasingly enlightened attitudes of learned authorities, amongst the general population fear of witchcraft persisted well into the nineteenth century and Victorian folklorists recorded countless such narratives in their county collections.

North Yorkshire was blessed with two prodigious collectors of witch lore during this period: Reverend J.C. Atkinson of Danby and Richard Blakeborough of Ripon, whose books provide a relatively reliable and comprehensive survey of witch belief in rural North Yorkshire at the time. Fear of maleficium causing injury to individuals does not seem to have been as rife as it was during the seventeenth century, doubtless helped by improved understanding of the causes of illness. Nonetheless, witches were still widely credited with the ability to adversely affect somebody's fortune and their livelihood. Equally, they were still identified with outsiders in the community, especially the friendless or destitute, who have always acted as scapegoats for any misfortune and were perceived to leech on the prosperity of the more industrious.

It is, therefore, not surprising that one of the principle crimes witches were imagined to commit was milk-stealing. In rural communities, dairy-farming was one of the cornerstones of the private economy and the subsistence of a household greatly depended upon its herd, so when the cows produced less than their expected yield for natural reasons such as infertility or mastitis, a scapegoat was required. Moreover, as J.C. Atkinson observes, prior to the passing of the Enclosure Acts between 1750 and 1860, livestock was grazed on common pasture and milk-stealing was a genuine problem which resulted in numerous court actions. Doubtless if a culprit could not be identified, then blame would be projected onto a witch.

Witches were ascribed the power of shape-shifting and supposed to go about their milk-stealing business in a variety of animal guises. Nancy Newgill of Broughton, for instance, not only changed into the form of a hedgehog and sucked the milk from cows' udders overnight; she also had power over other hedgehogs in the district to encourage them to do the same. Meanwhile, shortly after the herd belonging to a farmer at Alcomden above Calderdale ran dry, he woke in the night to find a strange black cat watching him for the end of his bed. He threw a knife at the intruder and struck its foreleg, which caused it to scamper away. The following day a neighbour remarked that he had seen old Sally Walton of Clough Foot near Widdop with her arm in a sling, and the farmer understood who had been bewitching his cattle in the night.

However, the milk-stealing, shape-shifting witch was most commonly associated with the hare. Like hedgehogs, hares are solitary, nocturnal feeding animals which might often have been seen in pastures after dark; unlike hedgehogs, they have a connection with magic extending into the pre-Christian past and an uncanny countenance that can disarm many. When a farmer in Commondale near Guisborough feared that a witch named 'Au'd Molly' was milking his cattle dry, he received advice to watch overnight in the field and carry a shotgun loaded with silver bullets, for nothing else could disable such a supernatural creature. But upon its arrival in the field, the witch-hare stalked up to the farmer and gave him such a stare with its piercing eyes that he turned heel and fled!

Sometimes the hare is not the witch herself but her familiar, albeit one with which the sorcerer is so intimately connected that injury to it has a corresponding effect on its mistress. This was the case at Eskdale where a drove of hares were causing great mischief by feeding on the saplings in a new plantation. The steward managed to cull them all except for one, which continued to evade both hound and bullet; he was subsequently advised to use silver slugs in his gun and with this contingency he finally succeeded in putting an end to the beast. At that moment, some distance away, an old woman with an evil reputation flung up her hands as she was carding wool and cried, 'They have shot my familiar spirit!' whereupon she fell to the floor dead.

The witch does not seem to have taken the form of a hare only to steal milk; in many tales, she seems to adopt such a guise for the sheer pleasure of it. In an archetypal narrative from Westerdale on the North York Moors, a party of hare-coursers encounter a witch simply known as 'Nanny'. She asks them how their sport is going and when the men reply that they haven't seen a single hare all day, she tells them of a field in which they might find just such an animal, one bound to give them a fine chase. They must only promise that they will not hunt it with a black dog. All members of the party agree to this stipulation and Nanny proceeds to tell them where this superior specimen of a leporid can be found.

Sure enough, the party find the hare in the place Nanny described, and they pursue it the length and breadth of the dale, never gaining upon it. But just as they are once more drawing near to the point where they started, a stray black dog joins the chase. It proves fleeter than any of their hounds and so little by little, it closes in on the hare until they reach the vicinity of Nanny's cottage. The hare makes straight for a cavity in the cottage walls but squeezes through it just a little too late, as the black dog manages to bite a chunk out of the hare's flank before it can get fully into the hole. The party of coursers is mortified: they know and fear Nanny's reputation, and are concerned about how she will react if she finds out that her injunction was broken, so they enter her cottage to explain. Within, they find Nanny lying on her bed, bleeding profusely from a wound on her haunch.

The tale is told of many witches in several different localities, such as Peg Humphreys of Bilsdale or Peggy Flaunders of Marske-by-the-Sea. Indeed, it is a classic example of a migratory legend known throughout the British Isles and much of northern Europe, the motif now categorised by folklorists as 'The Witch Who Was Hurt'. In Yorkshire, there are some minor local variations worth mentioning. For instance, the witch Abigail Craister, who dwelled in a cave on Black Hambleton, is said to have evaded pursuit by leaping from Whitestone Cliff into the waters of Gormire Lake below and re-emerged from a sinkhole some nine miles away. Her ghost is thought to haunt the vicinity of the lake still and can be seen riding over Kilburn on her broomstick.

Gormire Lake, haunted by the ghost of the witch Abigail Craister. (Kai Roberts)

However, the most developed and instructive version of the legend is told about Lady Sybil of Bearnshaw Tower in Cliviger, West Yorkshire. As a wealthy heiress, Lady Sybil was widely courted by suitors keen to lay their hands on her estates but unfortunately for them, Sybil was fond of her own company and her position was secure enough to rebut them all. Despite her repeated rejections, one suitor was more persistent than the rest: William Towneley was his name and he hailed from Hapton, near Burnley in Lancashire. Seeking to improve his chances, he sought advice from Mother Helston, a local wise-woman who intimated that she and Lady Sybil had much in common and rather than provide William with a simple love charm, directed him to go hunting around Thieveley Pike on All Hallows' Eve.

William followed Mother Helston's advice and sure enough he encountered a white doe of rare pedigree, which proceeded to run his hounds ragged across the moor. Eventually, they cornered the beast at a precipitous projection of rock known locally as Eagle Crag and William was able to slip a silk leash around its neck, as specified by the wise-woman. He led the doe back to the stables of his family seat at Hapton and the following morning was amazed to discover Lady Sybil sat where he had left it, with the silk leash still tied around her neck. With her secret discovered and prejudice against witchcraft being what it was, Lady Sybil was left with no option but to assent to William's proposal of marriage, lest he reveal her true nature.

Although Sybil initially agreed to renounce her sorcerous ways for the sake of the marriage, she soon grew restless and yearned to run wild over the lonely hills

Eagle Crag above Cliviger, burial place of Lady Sybil. (Kai Roberts)

around her old home once more. Increasingly, William found her missing from their bed during the night as she roamed the Cliviger district in the guise of a white cat. This particular feline, however, was not much liked in the neighbourhood as it riled up the other mousers and was often caught stealing milk from the dairy. One evening, a local miller decided to put an end to its visits and told his son to lay in wait for the animal overnight. When the cat finally arrived, the boy pounced; but whilst he managed to cut off one of its paws in the struggle, it escaped before he had the chance to kill it, leaving its severed paw behind.

The following morning, William Towneley found his wife confined to her bed-chamber with a terrible fever and blood-soaked sheets. Only when a mystified miller arrived from Cliviger, bearing a severed female hand with a distinctive ring on one of its fingers, did he understand what had occurred. Fortunately, although she was weak from loss of blood, Lady Sybil was able to use her magical art to reattach the appendage. Nonetheless, she bore an ugly red circle around her wrist thereafter and never again went roving the moors. She died barely a year after the event and as her witchery was now widely known, she was refused burial in consecrated ground. Instead, she was interred at the foot of Eagle Crag and it is said that on Halloween, a spectral doe pursued by phantom hounds can be seen bounding across the moors thereabouts.

It seems especially clear from the Cliviger version of 'The Witch Who Was Hurt' legend that the motif was an expression of the gender politics of its age. In narratives where the witch adopts an animal guise simply for the joy of it, her crime is not maleficium but daring to exhibit independence. Such tales symbolise the forcible 'taming' of headstrong, autonomous women by patriarchal forces, threatening the unfortunate consequences which may befall such individuals if they fail to adhere to gender norms and submit to male authority, whether it be social opprobrium or physical injury. Although it is simplistic to say that all fear of witchcraft arose from historical misogynistic attitudes, 'The Witch Who Was Hurt' undoubtedly displays profound hostility towards the possibility of liberated women.

There is no evidence for the existence of any Lady Sybil at Bearnshaw Tower, but often such migratory legends were attached to historical individuals for whom this must have represented a considerable danger. Nan Hardwick was a Danby woman with a reputation for witchcraft and it was her habit to spend evenings sat amongst the gorse on a bank about a mile from her cottage. No reason is given for her behaviour but it was regarded as 'aberrant' by the local community and as such, young men used to play a game they called 'Hunt Auld Nan Hardwick'. It is said that on an evening in Danby her clogged feet were often heard rattling along the causey from the gorse bank to her home, with a pack of baying hounds and jeering youths in hot pursuit.

Nor were the acts attributed to such women always so benign as shape-shifting, and many were accused of maleficium in local legend. Peggy Flaunders of Marske-by-the-Sea, who died in 1835 aged eighty-five, was believed to hold a grudge against a local farmer named Tom Pearson and when all his cattle died, she was blamed for bewitching them. Pearson was ruined and forced to sell his land to a cousin who had always been civil to Peggy. It is said that on the morning he took possession of the farm, she walked past and wished him well, before performing a curious ritual: she turned around three times, threw her cloak on the ground and leapt over it whilst muttering some incantation. The farm proceeded to prosper under its new owner.

A more sinister story is told of Auld Nanny of Ayrton, who according to Richard Blakeborough lived around the district sometime between 1750 and 1780. Mary Longstaffe of Stokesley was in Kildale to nurse her unwell cousin, Martha Sokeld and one day noticed the ill-favoured old woman hobbling towards her. To avoid conversation, Mary feigned picking some flowers from the verge but unfortunately for both Mary and her cousin, Nanny noticed this snub and took offence. The alleged witch said she would not forget the insult, banged the ground thrice with her stick and disappeared. As Mary was wearing a sprig of rowan at the time, which provided protection from witch-work, she thought little of the encounter and a few days later when her cousin had regained her health, she returned to her home in Stokesley.

Several nights later, Mary was surprised when Martha turned up at her home. She claimed to have taken a turn for the worse and would not live much longer, so she was travelling to Northallerton to bid farewell to her sister. She asked Martha if she could stay with her in Stokesley for the night before journeying on the following day. Mary agreed, and Martha sent her out for some items she wanted whilst she napped. Martha seemed so eager to be rid of her that Mary grew uneasy and returned before her time to spy through the window. To her horror, she saw her kinswoman dropping powders into a pan over the fire whilst muttering some incantation, at which point Mary realised that it was not Martha but Nanny in her cousin's guise. She rushed and struck Nanny with a Bible, causing the witch to throw over the pan and flee. The next day, news came from Kildale that Martha Sokeld's body had been found on the moors, three days dead.

Whilst Mary Longstaffe was fortunate enough to have interrupted the spell-casting before it could take effect, others were not so lucky and many stories suggest that it required considerable effort to ward off the effects of maleficium once it had been directed at them. Typically the blood of the witch was needed to neutralise the spell, which was not an easy thing to procure: often it had to be taken whilst the witch was in animal guise and even then certain procedures had to be followed before the creature could be caught. In some cases, these measures were familiar. For example, when the squire of Goathland called on Nanny Pearson to bewitch his daughter to prevent her eloping with a suitor of whom he disapproved, a wise-man advised the young lover to track the witch as a hare and shoot it with silver bullets to obtain the essential ingredient for a counter-spell.

In other instances, the instructions were more opaque. The folklorist William Henderson records that a Halifax man charged with obtaining blood from a local witch named Auld Betty was told to bake a cake before the fire of the household she was enchanting. This he did, and at length he noticed a black cat sitting by the fire, although he did not see or hear it enter. He was surprised to hear a voice from the cat purr 'Cake burns' to which he replied, 'Turn it then.' After a little while, the cat made the same complaint and the witch-catcher gave the same answer. This exchanged went on again and again, until the man grew so frustrated that he forgot that he had been warned against uttering any holy names in the witch's presence and he responded with an oath. At the sound of this, the cat mewled and sprang up the chimney with the witch-catcher in hot pursuit. He emerged badly mauled but managed to wound the animal with a table fork and the bewitchment was undone.

A belief in the efficacy of the witch's blood in counter-spells was evidently deeply ingrained in the Calderdale region. As late as 1904, a local antiquary noted that people believed that victims of witchcraft only needed to scratch their tormentor's back with a pin to break her hold over them. Two and a half centuries earlier, the Heptonstall witch trial intimated similar superstitions were held. It records that the minister of Cross Stones Chapel told Daniel Briggs of Wadsworth that if he wished to break the suspected bewitchment of a neighbour's child, if anybody crossed his path on his way home, he should 'maul them in the head'. Briggs did in fact meet Elizabeth Crossley on his return journey, who suspiciously inquired after the health of the infant; but whilst Briggs was too afraid to act himself, the following day his maid attacked Crossley with a candlestick.

In many cases, it was the local wise-man or wise-woman who provided counsel when it came to combating maleficium. These individuals were sometimes referred to as 'cunning folk', derived from the Old English 'cunna' meaning 'to know' and indeed, knowledge was their most successful commodity. Such people were often literate in a widely uneducated society and tended to be well versed in arts such as astrology and herbalism. Yet cunning folk possessed an ambivalent reputation. Whilst their learned advice was often widely sought after, they were still regarded as being only a step away from witches themselves and should relations with a client turn sour, their position was tenuous. Equally, many stories circulated to suggest that they should not be trifled with – possibly propagated by the cunning folk themselves.

In some respects, people were right to fear cunning folk as the awe in which they were held provided the perfect cloak for nefarious deeds and whilst they may not have practiced maleficium through sorcery, they undoubtedly practiced it through more orthodox means. The infamous example here is Mary Bateman of Leeds, who used her reputation as a wise-woman to poison at least three clients and obtain their property. She was finally caught when the coroner investigating the death of her third victim found evidence of arsenic in the deceased's stomach and with the help of the woman's husband entrapped Bateman, who was passing off arsenic-laced concoctions as healing potions. Bateman was executed on 20 March 1809 and such was her reputation as a witch, her skin was tanned and her tongue pickled to be sold to those who wished to exploit their supposed supernatural power.

On the other hand, some cunning folk were certainly held in great esteem and John Wrightson, known as the Wise Man of Stokesley, was one such example. Wrightson died in 1840, but remembrances collected later by J.C. Atkinson and Richard Blakeborough suggest he was favourably regarded by all who'd had dealings with him. His methods seem to have been a potent mix of showmanship, charlatanry, herbalism and canny insight into human nature – he maintained a network of informants to keep him apprised of local gossip and like many modern fortune-tellers, he was probably adept at cold-reading. Wrightson also undoubtedly cultivated his image, claiming to be the seventh son of a seventh son and receiving clients in a room full of esoteric paraphernalia whilst wearing a long gown and strange headgear.

Numerous stories about Wrightson's powers have been recorded. Some are perfectly explicable – such as his successful diagnosis of tumour in a cow – whilst others have probably been exaggerated to enhance his reputation, especially those which emphasise his powers of precognition and mesmerism. One tale relates that as two young men were passing close to his house, they thought to have a little fun with Wrightson and so called to see him. He received them warmly enough, told them to take seats by the fire and proceeded to engage them in conversation about all manner of topics, during which time he placed log after log on the hearth. After a while, the two men grew uncomfortably hot, but when they tried to move away from the fire, they found themselves paralysed in their seats. They endured this ordeal for some time before Wrightson decided they had learnt their lesson and sent the pair away with a reprimand for their impudence in thinking they could toy with him.

Another credited with second sight was the Wise Woman of Littondale, who lived in a rundown cottage near Arncliffe filled with black cats and pictures of Merlin, Michael Scott and Nostradamus. When a sceptic visited her to seek proof of her power, she is said to have shown him a vision of one of his friends in her scrying vessel and told him to wait alone at Arncliffe Bridge at midnight. The man followed her instructions and at the foretold hour heard a low moan and saw a great disturbance in the waters below. As he returned home, he encountered a great black dog which vanished as mysteriously as it had appeared. The following day this man returned to the Wise Woman to ask the meaning of these things. She told him that the dog he'd seen was a barguest and despite his scepticism, the man knew such an encounter portended death. Later in the day, he was told that the friend whose image he'd seen in the scrying glass had committed suicide from Arncliffe Bridge that very morning.

If the famed Mother Shipton of Knaresborough was a historical figure, it is likely that her reputation during her lifetime was as a cunning-woman with powers of precognition. Her alleged prophecies were almost certainly fabricated by later writers in order to feed the seventeenth-century appetite for such material, but it is possible that they were inspired by an older oral tradition. In 1684, Richard Head recorded biographical details, claiming that she was born Ursula Southiel around 1488 in a cave on the banks of the River Nidd and adopted the name Mother Shipton following her marriage to Toby Shipton in 1521. However, as she is supposed to have died in 1561 and documentary record of her name does not appear until the first publication of her supposed prophecies in 1642, the evidence for her historical existence is thin.

Nonetheless, between the seventeenth and nineteenth century, her reputation as a soothsayer was unassailable across the whole of England. Following the publication of *Two Strange Prophecies* in 1642, interest burgeoned so rapidly that the pamphlet had expanded to *Fourteen Strange Prophecies* by 1649. The celebrated diarist, Samuel Pepys even records that during the Great Fire of London in 1666, the king's cousin, Prince Rupert, was heard to remark, 'Now Shipton's prophecy is out.' This was in reference to a notorious couplet which ran, 'Triumphant Death rides London through / And men on tops of houses go'. Typically, however, like most prophecies, Mother Shipton's alleged divinations are couched in ambiguous, symbolic language and for any event, there are lines which can be imagined to fit.

With the success of the prophecies, a rich body of legend grew up around Mother Shipton's birth and supposed childhood in Knaresborough. It was said that she was born from her mother's union with the Devil and that fearsome sounds accompanied her entry into the world. Even as an infant, Ursula was reported to be fearsomely ugly, with a crooked body, hooked nose and goggling eyes. Her powers manifested from an early age and she would make the furniture in her nurse's house dance up and down the stairs. On one occasion, the child went missing and when her nurse returned with a search party, they were all magically compelled to take the four ends of a cross and dance until they dropped, whilst a simian imp goaded them with pins. A priest was eventually summoned and he found Ursula in her cradle, floating three full yards above the ground.

Mother Shipton's fame endures today, as the cave in which she was purportedly born has been turned into one of North Yorkshire's principle tourist attractions – although arguably its appeal rests on the neighbouring petrifying well rather than the cave itself. Nonetheless, the sibyl has become something of a county icon, which may be some small vindication for all those who were persecuted for their uncanny reputation in Yorkshire's history. Her birthplace is certainly a more edifying spectacle than the skeleton of Mary Bateman, which following the donation of her corpse to an anatomy school after her execution now hangs forlorn in the Thackerary Medical Museum – a stark reminder of the havoc superstition could wreak in centuries gone by.

TWO

CHARMS AND
TALISMANS

Before the advance of modern science, when livelihoods could be destroyed
by a simple crop blight and lives suddenly snatched away by some unknown
sickness, so many individuals must have felt cast adrift in a hostile environment,
powerless against forces beyond their understanding or control. With the human
tendency to anthropomorphise and seek causal agency, the world could not help
but be transformed into a demon-haunted place, apparently overrun by baleful
supernatural forces bent on doing harm to persons and property. It is scarcely
surprising that these beleaguered folk attempted to assert control by any means
necessary, and a rich legacy of protective charms and talismans survives as testament
to their endeavour. Whilst such contingencies may seem absurd today, they once
represented the only hope in the face of an unforgiving universe.

Should a house find itself tormented by a restless spirit, there were few
expedients available following the Reformation, as the rite of exorcism was
forbidden to Protestant clergy and often householders were forced to resort to
a local cunning-person to help 'lay' the ghost. Such individuals might perform a
corrupted remembrance of the old Catholic ritual or provide a charm to ward off
the spirit, which had to be kept in the house indefinitely. For instance, in 1905, the
occupier of High Fernley Hall at Wyke in West Yorkshire discovered seven pieces
of parchment concealed in the rafters of the building, apparently deliberately fixed
into place for posterity. These parchments were inscribed in the legal hand of the
latter half of the eighteenth century, each with a series of largely nonsensical words
doubtless meant as magical formulae.

It was locally believed that the charm had been placed to offer protection against
the ghost of a former owner of the hall, who had committed suicide there. Legends

record that in the mid-eighteenth century, High Fernley Hall was occupied by two
brothers named Bevers, both of whom loved the same woman. Only one brother
won the lady's affection, however, and they were married at Kirkheaton Church
on 5 May 1742. After witnessing the ceremony, the spurned suitor returned to High
Fernley, whereupon he told the servants that tragedy would soon befall him and
he would 'come again' minus his head. He then proceeded to take his own life,
supposedly by decapitating himself, although this might be a later embellishment to
account for the condition of his ghost.

Sure enough, the unfortunate Bevers brother returned every night as a headless
horseman, galloping up and down the lane which led from High Fernley Hall
to Judy Woods. Few locals dared walk that way after dark and the house stood
untenanted for many years, until that portion in which the suicide had taken place
was demolished. Considering the apparent agreement between the date of the
suicide and the approximate date of the parchment charms, it seems highly likely
that they were intended to ward off Bevers' acephalous spectre. Following their
rediscovery in 1905, a local belief developed that bad luck would befall the hall and
its tenants should the charms ever be removed.

Of course, the majority of household talismans between the sixteenth and
nineteenth century were intended as a defence against witchcraft – specifically
maleficium. In some cases, they were purely prophylactic; designed to protect
against potential witchcraft, rather than a spell already directed against the house
(which typically needed stronger measures to undo). The most common example,
known throughout the British Isles, was a horseshoe nailed to the door of the
house. In his 1686 work, *Remains of Gentilism and Judaism*, the antiquarian John
Aubrey noted that the power of horseshoes derived from the fact they were made
of iron; although it is not clear why most sources insisted that their points should be
directed upwards. Nonetheless, positioned thus, no witch could cross the threshold
and their spells would be reflected back upon them.

Similarly effective were stones through which a natural hole had been bored.
This occurred as the result of water action over many centuries and such pebbles
were usually plucked from the seashore or a streambed. Known variously as holy-
stones, hag-stones or dobby-stones, smaller examples were kept about the person
as a portable talisman – often attached to a door-key; whilst larger specimens were
hung in the home or sometimes in stables. It was widely believed that witches stole
horses and rode them hard to their sabbats, before returning them to their stalls
sweating and exhausted. Animals found in such a condition were described as 'hag-
ridden' and the holed stone was regarded as an effective defence against this danger.

The wood of the rowan tree (sometimes known as mountain ash) was also
thought to protect against witchcraft and being easier to come by than horseshoes
and holed stones, it was very extensively deployed. Sprigs of rowan were hung in
each room of the house; in the stables and byres, above the beds, behind every
window and door. On farms it was considered prudent to make the churn-staff

A sprig of rowan, hung
to protect a house from
witches. (Kai Roberts)

and whip-stocks from rowan wood, whilst it was tied around the horns or necks
of cattle to keep them safe from maleficium. Some cottages even went so far as to
have a rowan tree growing in their garden to hold the witches at bay. Beyond the
home, people would wear posies in their buttonholes, carry twigs in their pockets
and place leaves in their shoes.

In some areas of the county, cutting rowan for such use had to be performed with
the appropriate ritual. Around Cleveland, St Helen's Day (2 May) was the appointed
time for this ceremony. Householders would rise before dawn and proceed into
the woods to search for a suitable tree. For the rowan charm to be fully effective,
the wood had to be cut with a domestic knife and taken from a tree of which the
cutter had no previous knowledge. In Holderness, meanwhile, the rowan had to
be gathered at a certain times of day to be fully effective. Noon was considered
relatively favourable, but wood procured at midnight was thought to be the most
potent – especially when fashioned into the shape of a cross.

Rowan was also used to make witch-posts, an architectural feature unique to
North Yorkshire farmhouses in the sixteenth and seventeenth century, especially
around Farndale. These thick wooden posts were usually located beside the hearth
to protect the threshold from unwelcome incursion. The chimney was regarded as
a common access point for witches during the night, but such intruders could not
pass beyond a rowan witch-post. For additional security, their faces were carved
with a St Andrew's Cross, beneath which were a number of lines believed to
represent the number of people in the household requiring protection. Sometimes
a crooked sixpence was stored in a niche in the centre of the post and if the butter
would not emulsify due to some enchantment laid upon it, the sixpence was taken
from this position and placed in the churn as a counter-spell.

But such techniques were only good as preventative measures; if maleficium was
already directed at the household, more evasive action was required. In such cases,
the local cunning-person was again the resort of choice and often counter-attack

A witch-post preserved from a Farndale farmhouse. (Kai Roberts)

was their recommended course of action. The principle by which maleficium was thought to operate required that the witch establish an intimate connection with the target of their spite; hence why the personal affects of a victim were often needed to direct the spell. However, this connection could be fruitfully turned against the witch so that in order to escape her own suffering, she would be forced to undo the original enchantment.

For instance, when the dairy was thought to be bewitched and the butter would not churn, it was imagined that sticking a red-hot poker into the cream would be quickly felt by the witch. More elaborately, when a farmer living near Skipton in the eighteenth century believed his cattle to be bewitched, a local wise-man instructed him that on a specified day he was to kindle a fire behind his house and gather his family round. They were then to take the heart from one of the diseased cows and boil it in a pan suspended over the fire; when the organ was removed, each member of the family was to stick a pin into it. The next stage of the procedure varied: sometimes the heart was burnt on the fire; sometimes it was placed in the chimney; and sometimes it was buried in consecrated ground.

When an individual was suffering from an illness believed to be the result of maleficium, a witch-bottle was used. Typically, the hair, fingernails and urine of the target was placed with a great quantity of pins or nails in an earthenware jar which was then heated over a fire. Again, it was believed that the link an enchantment established between a witch and her victim was such that this tactic would cause great pain to her. It was imagined she would feel the heat from the fire and the symbolic stabbing of the pins, and she would be forced to reverse the initial spell to spare herself this agony. Her only other hope of release was for the jar to shatter during the heating process or if she could get to it herself and destroy it.

Often this would also have the effect of identifying the malefactor. One story relates that when the child of a Halifax family fell ill, the above procedure was followed and the witch-bottle was left to heat on the fire overnight. During the early hours of the morning, there was a rap at the door and outside stood the notorious Auld Betty in an evident state of distress. She asked if they needed their fire 'riddling' (to sieve out the ash) but unfortunately such a transparent attempt to access the house and destroy the witch-bottle was immediately recognised. She was chased from the door and shortly thereafter, the child began to recover, suggesting Auld Betty had been forced to lift her spell.

A typical witch-bottle was unearthed around 1960 at Halton East, near Skipton, buried upside down in a field, apparently far from the nearest habitation. It was found to hold several lumps of clay, each one pierced through; altogether there were thirty-five pins, twenty-two nails and sixteen needles. This location was unusual, however. More often witch-bottles were placed in the fabric of the building or beneath the threshold to preserve the household from further mischief and they have frequently been discovered in such contexts many years later. A particularly unique example was discovered in the 1970s, buried beneath the doorstep of an outbuilding attached to a seventeenth-century farmhouse at Ogden, near Halifax. The jar contained some form of liquid, which could well have been urine, and two fragile clay figurines, doubtless intended to represent the bewitched individuals.

A witch-bottle discovered at Ogden near Halifax. (Kai Roberts)

It is quite common for other magically protective artefacts to be found in the fabric of old buildings, especially near threshold locations such as doorways, windows, chimneys and eaves. Such items are described as 'apotropaic' meaning 'to ward off evil'. Amongst the most common discoveries were old shoes, which have been turned up in such large quantities and in such unusual locations that accidental deposition can be ruled out. Nobody has yet produced a convincing explanation as to why old shoes were regarded as an appropriate defence against evil. In a study of apotropaic practices, archaeologist Ralph Merrifield suggested that they were 'considered an effective trap for an evil spirit', based on a fourteenth-century legend concerning a Buckinghamshire priest who cast the Devil into an old boot.

Not quite as ubiquitous but rather more memorable is the desiccated cat. These are usually discovered in airtight cavities in the walls of seventeenth-century buildings, where they were deliberately placed and allowed to starve or suffocate. Sometimes they have even been fixed in position to simulate a cat on the hunt. It is not entirely clear how widespread this practice was, as such finds are inadequately recorded. Often workmen assume they were simply an animal that got trapped and dispose of them; or else, understanding their possible significance, replace them in the wall when the work is complete. Nonetheless, it appears that it was not a purely secular custom, as a desiccated cat was discovered in the roof of the Church of St Thomas a Becket at Heptonstall when it was demolished in 1875.

Again, the exact function of desiccated cats remains debatable. Some deflationary historians have suggested they were merely intended to deter rats and mice. However, as Ralph Merrifield notes, 'As such it was hardly less superstitious, with its quasi-magical imitation of a hunting cat. It is also possible that the real fear underlying the practice was spiritual rather than actual rodents.' It was a familiar principle of magical thinking that 'like affects like' and considering the preference of witches for feline familiars, people may have believed a totem cat represented the building's best defence against such attack. This would certainly explain why desiccated cats are found at vulnerable threshold points such as chimneys and roofs.

The use of desiccated cats has also been associated with the practice of foundation sacrifice. There is abundant archaeological evidence to suggest that nearly all the pre-Christian cultures of the British Isles made ritual offerings to guarantee the fortune of a new building, the remains of which were typically deposited in the foundations. Animals were the most common sacrifice, and the placing of horse-skulls in this context continued for many centuries – as another discovery at Halton East attests. But there are also indications that humans were occasionally used in such a fashion; and whilst such grisly practices are often thought to be a relic of pagan superstition, the principle of foundation sacrifice may have persisted well into the Middle Ages.

In 1895, renovation work was undertaken on the medieval tower of St Luke and All Saints' Church at Darrington, near Pontefract, following damage during a storm. The *Yorkshire Herald* reported:

It was found that under the west side of the tower, only about a foot from the surface, the body of a man had been placed in a sort of bed in the solid rock, and the west wall was actually resting on his skull ... The grave must have been prepared and the wall placed with deliberate intention upon the head of the person buried, and this was done with such care that all remained as placed for at least six hundred years.

Although this individual may not have been deliberately killed for the purpose, it certainly suggests that the power of human remains to ensure the luck of a building did not die out with the conversion of Britain to Christianity.

Indeed, the cult of relics was an archetypal feature of medieval Catholicism and whilst this orthodox doctrine may not have extended to the apotropaic use of human remains in secular contexts, there was undoubtedly a continuum between the two. Yorkshire has several examples of human skulls being used for apotropaic purposes and although these traditions primarily seem to date from the seventeenth century and beyond, it is possible that their roots go much deeper. The use of the skull as opposed to any other bone is easy enough to understand; many cultures regard the skull as the seat of the soul and there is extensive evidence to suggest that the image of the head itself is frequently considered apotropaic in magical thinking. Certainly it reinforces the image of watchful guardianship and such relics are often referred to as 'guardian skulls'.

Burton Agnes Hall in East Yorkshire, home of a guardian skull known as Owd Nance. (Kai Roberts)

The most famous example in the county is the skull known as 'Owd Nance', kept at Burton Agnes Hall in East Yorkshire. Local folklore relates that this mansion was built during the reign of Elizabeth I by three sisters named Frances, Margaret and Anne Griffith. Anne was the youngest and the most enthusiastic about the project, but tragically before the building was complete, she was attacked by robbers whilst travelling home one night and mortally wounded. On her death bed, she made her surviving sisters promise that following her death they would remove her skull and give it a position of honour in the new Hall. Frances and Margaret solemnly agreed to Anne's request, but failed to fulfil the vow once she had passed away.

As a result, their lives were made a misery for the next two years as their new home was wracked by terrible moans and other uncanny noises. No servant would remain in their employment and eventually they were forced to have their late sister's corpse exhumed. Her skull was removed and placed on a table in a position of honour in the Hall. The belief developed that as long as 'Owd Nance' remained undisturbed, the building and its occupants would enjoy good fortune. However, should the skull be displaced or slighted in any way, dire consequences were sure to follow. One story claims that a maid, sick of the skull's macabre presence and sceptical of its supposed power, threw the offending item on a loaded wagon outside. At once 'the horses plunged and reared, the house shook, pictures fell,' and the skull was returned to its proper position forthwith.

Owd Nance's unnerving visage was never particularly appreciated by the residents of Burton Agnes and during the nineteenth century, Sir Henry Boynton (a descendant of the Griffith sisters) had it bricked up in the wall, ensuring that it could no longer disturb the residents, nor could it ever be removed. The precise location of the skull today remains a closely guarded secret, although it is variously believed to be above a doorway in one of the upper corridors, or behind the fireplace of the Queen's State bedroom in the north wing. The latter room is also rumoured to be haunted by a ghost thought to be that of Owd Nance. According to one source, 'She still appears occasionally and generally in the month of October, which is supposed to have been the month of her death. She is short, slight and dressed in fawn colour.'

The only difficulty is that whilst the existence of the skull is never doubted, the legend of its origin appears to be entirely fictitious. Burton Agnes Hall was built in 1601 for Sir Henry Griffith and besides a portrait of dubious provenance known as 'The Three Miss Griffiths', there is no historical record of an Anne Griffiths in the family during this period. It raises the possibility that the skull may have been a much older relic brought to Burton Agnes by the Griffith family when they moved from their native Wales in the thirteenth century. There would certainly be precedent for such a conclusion: the guardian skull kept at Bettiscombe Manor in Dorset, which local tradition asserted belonged to a West Indian servant who worked there during the seventeenth century, actually proved to be the remains of a prehistoric woman, some three to four thousand years old.

Sowood House, where a guardian skull was uncovered in the 1960s. (Kai Roberts)

Although Burton Agnes is the most famous case, several other examples of guardian skulls exist in Yorkshire and bad luck invariably follows their removal. During the early nineteenth century, a skull was discovered in a lead box concealed behind the fireplace of Sowood House at Coley, near Halifax. It was given a Christian burial in the local churchyard, but the tenants of Sowood were subsequently disturbed by nocturnal cries of 'Where's my head?' and forced to return the skull to its original position to bring the trouble to an end. Unfortunately, the skull was revealed yet again during renovations in the 1960s and passed to the police for investigation, since which time its whereabouts have been impossible to ascertain. A specimen was also recorded at Lund Manor House in East Yorkshire, but this too was walled up and no narratives relating to it survive.

Traditions continue to be attached to such artefacts even in the modern period. Hull's Ye Olde White Harte Inn has a skull on permanent display in its bar, believed to have been discovered at the hostelry in the late nineteenth century. It appears to have belonged to a youth and a fracture in the bone suggests its owner may have died from a blunt blow to the head. Various stories have arisen to account for this fact: one version suggests the skull belonged to a boy who was murdered by a drunken sea captain and his body concealed under the staircase; another account claims the skull is that of a serving maid who maybe committed suicide or was murdered following a liaison with the landlord and her corpse concealed in the attic. Either way, it is believed bad luck will befall the pub should the skull ever be removed from the building.

An archaic stone head at Coley Hall near Halifax. (Kai Roberts)

In another example, in the late nineteenth century, Lord Halifax placed three skulls – believed to be former medical specimens – in a glass case beside the lych-gate at St Wilfrid's Church in Hickleton, South Yorkshire. He intended them to serve as a *memento mori* and reinforced this function by having the legend 'Today For Me, Tomorrow For Thee' inscribed beneath. Yet a hundred years later, their original purpose had been forgotten in the village and local tradition now associated them with three highwaymen who had been gibbeted at a nearby crossroads. When the glass case was smashed and one of the skulls stolen in 1996, even the vicar of St Wilfrid's gave voice to the local feeling that the skulls were cursed and misfortune would befall anybody who removed them from their rightful position at the church.

The apotropaic role of the human skull also has echoes in one of the most individual features of Yorkshire folk art: the archaic stone head. These carvings of human heads are referred to as 'archaic' as they appear to have been deliberately carved in a crude, almost primitive style, even where the mason was clearly capable of more sophisticated work. The face is typically flat and almost two-dimensional: the eyes are round or oval and often bulging; the nose is little more than a triangle in relief; and the mouth a mere hole or groove. Other features such as ears and hair occasionally appear, but always rendered in the same rudimentary style. As such, these carvings seem intended to represent not any historical individual, or mythological figure, but a universal archetype of the human head.

It is similarly evident that they were not designed as decorative motifs. Often the appearance of these carvings is quite disconcerting and they are frequently found in locations where they are impossible to see without great effort. Furthermore, they are almost exclusively positioned at 'liminal' points. Liminality describes locations which are betwixt and between, neither one place nor the other, the point where a defined space is divided from the next – boundaries, thresholds, margins, borders and so forth. But to a holistic worldview, which perceives the material and non-material realm as intrinsically entangled, liminal places are not just boundaries and thresholds in the physical world alone. They are also places where our world presses close against the Other and as such, are especially vulnerable to incursions from beyond.

In the household, doors, windows, chimneys, roofs, gables and gateways are classic liminal points; whilst outdoors, field boundaries, water-crossings and wells are regarded similarly. Clearly such vulnerable spots required magical protection against malevolent supernatural intrusion and the fact that archaic stone heads are found exclusively in these places indicates that their purpose was primarily apotropaic. Although no study of such features was made until the mid-twentieth century, this hypothesis was confirmed by what few narrative traditions remained connected with the carvings. Where local people did hold an opinion on the function of an archaic stone head in their neighbourhood, they were most often believed to protect the structure against misfortune and malign influences.

Archaic stone heads were also sometimes believed to commemorate an individual who died during construction work or nearby, despite the carvings having few distinguishing features. It is possible that this belief may be a corrupted remembrance of the apotropaic function of foundation sacrifices, of which the stone head has become a symbolic representation. A classic example is carved on an aqueduct constructed in 1795, which carries the Rochdale Canal over the River Calder at Hebden Bridge. Local tradition claims it is a memorial to somebody who drowned in the river below whilst trying to rescue a child. However, it is almost impossible to see the carving from any vantage point other than the river itself – hardly a fitting monument. As the folklorist John Billingsley comments, the head 'appears to be directed at a supernatural rather than a human audience.'

Although archaic stone heads are found throughout the South Pennines, the greatest concentration of such features in vernacular architecture is found around the Aire and Calder valleys. Indeed, their significance was first noticed by Sidney Jackson, a curator working for Bradford Museums Service. Impressed by the contemporary work of Professor Anne Ross on the religious beliefs of Celtic Britain, Jackson grew convinced that many archaic stone heads were actually Celtic in origin, or at least represented an unbroken tradition of such carvings in the region since the Iron Age. Considering that West Yorkshire was the last independent Celtic territory in England – surviving until at least the seventh century before it was subsumed by the Anglo-Saxon kingdom of Northumbria – such speculation did not seem entirely improbable.

An archaic stone head on Agden Bridge in South Yorkshire. (Kai Roberts)

It is true that skulls and other representations of the human head were widely used as cultic objects by the Celts, and a number of the carved heads found in West Yorkshire do have an Iron Age or Romano-British provenance. Equally, many of the later examples bear a striking stylistic resemblance to the authentically Celtic specimens. Anne Ross herself noted when she surveyed a collection put together by Jackson, 'What strikes me as above all significant is not so much whether this head or that is genuinely Celtic or not, but the extraordinary continuity of culture shown by this collection. Presumably without knowing it, there are local craftsmen of this very century in these Yorkshire industrial valleys, carving heads with specific characteristics such as the "Celtic eye" … It is a treasure house of continuity.'

However, firm evidence of a continuing tradition is impossible to establish. The vast majority of heads seem to have been carved between the sixteenth and nineteenth century, whilst many others were not found in datable contexts. There are certainly no obvious examples from the early Middle Ages which could bolster the notion of an unbroken lineage and stylistic evidence alone is not sufficient to establish survival over a thousand years from the Dark Ages into the early modern period. As a result, the term 'archaic stone head' is now favoured over 'Celtic stone head' and most are regarded as the indigenous product of Yorkshire craftsmen during the period following the Reformation until the end of the Industrial Revolution.

Nonetheless, isolated instances of head carving for apotropaic purposes endured in West Yorkshire well into the twentieth century. In 1971, when the landlord and regulars of the Old Sun Inn at Haworth complained that their pub was being haunted by a disembodied voice, a local advised them to have a head carved and place it above the threshold. The landlord acted on this recommendation and an archaic stone head was fitted above the porch. Sure enough, the supernatural disturbances ceased and the head remains in place today. Even where the apotropaic function of such carvings has been forgotten, there is evidence that they are still being fashioned as part of a self-conscious revival of the vernacular architectural traditions of the region. Thus, however old the tradition may be, it may thrive for many years yet.

THREE

Dragons and Serpents

Today, we tend to think of dragons as mythical creatures that belong to the same category as demons, fairies and other such impossible entities. Their legends seem equally fanciful and their natures similarly super-natural. However, it is clear that our ancestors lacked any such association. As veteran folklorist Jacqueline Simpson notes in her study of the subject, 'There is no connection between dragons and those sites which are traditionally regarded as haunted, sinister or demonic, such as graveyards, gallows and gibbets, places where murders and suicides have occurred and so forth … Dragons were not categorised as part of the eerie world of supernatural spirits and demons that lurk in haunted, evil places.'

Whilst they may have thought dragons to be extinct in our own country, previous generations seemed to have had no doubt that such flesh-and-blood creatures had once infested the land and perhaps endured in certain remote parts of the globe. Nor was this belief confined to the uneducated classes; even scholarly commentators affirmed the existence of such beasts, as evinced by Edmund Topsell in his 1608 work, *The Historie of Serpents*, or Ulisse Aldrovandi's *Serpentum et Draconum* of 1640. Prior to the greater understanding of natural history which developed in the eighteenth and nineteenth centuries, this is not entirely surprising. Dragons are referred to in both Biblical and Classical sources, and such textual authority was once sufficient to endorse the truth of a matter.

Similarly, until palaeontology developed as a scientific discipline, the bones and fossilised prints of dinosaurs seemed to provide material evidence for the former existence of dragons. Indeed, until the fossil sequence was properly delineated and it became clear that dinosaurs were not contemporaneous with early humans, some writers wondered if dragons might not have been a race memory of those great

Castle Hill above Huddersfield, once home to a treasure-guarding dragon? (Kai Roberts)

reptiles. The issue was further compounded by the numerous fakes which were once displayed by travelling fairs and the like. Known as Jenny Hanivers, these specimens were actually dried sea creatures modified to resemble all manner of fantastical creatures, including dragons, but also mermaids, angels and devils.

Of course, tales of dragons have a long and illustrious pedigree in Britain. Known to the Anglo-Saxons as 'wyrms', dragons seem to have been a significant motif in their culture and an important portion of the eighth-century epic poem *Beowulf* revolves around an archetypal example of the beast. This treasure-guarding dragon has become the dominant image of the dragon in Western culture, probably through its use by J.R.R. Tolkien and subsequent assimilation into fantasy fiction. However, the dragons of English local legend rarely conform to this treasure-guardian type and beyond a few hints here and there, it seems as if the Anglo-Saxon tradition did not survive in the popular consciousness much beyond the Norman Conquest.

The hints which exist are tantalising but not conclusive, primarily stemming from the notoriously unreliable study of toponymy. For instance, on Cringle Moor in Cleveland there is a tumulus known as Drake Howe, the name of which is thought to derive from the Old English term for a dragon. There is also a legend that treasure is buried within the mound. However, no surviving narrative explicitly connects a dragon with the treasure, and as Chapter 11 shows, associations between ancient earthworks and treasure are not at all uncommon in Yorkshire, so this may have nothing to do with a dragon at all. Attempts have also been made to connect the legend of a 'Golden Cradle' buried in the earthworks of Castle Hill above Huddersfield to a dragon suggested by the nearby toponym 'Wyrmcliffe'.

However, as so many toponyms have been subject to centuries of consonantal drift, it is difficult to say with confidence to what it originally referred and a great deal of wishful thinking has been exhibited by amateur philologists over the years. An example of the controversial nature of such speculation can be seen in Reverend H.N. Pobjoy's attempt to derive the name of Blakelaw, a vanished hamlet that once stood on Hartshead Moor in West Yorkshire, from the Old English *Dracanhlawe*, meaning 'Mound of the Dragon'. He sought to connect this with vague rumours of a dragon legend he'd heard amongst the locals of his parish. Yet another, arguably more authoritative source, prefers to give it as *Blachelana*, which has the prosaic translation of 'black hill'.

Where detailed dragon legends do survive in Yorkshire, they all conform to a single type. These beasts are invariably voracious and destructive, but do not guard treasure. Nor does it take theft to incite them to terrorise the surrounding countryside – rather such aggression is intrinsic to their nature. Furthermore, whilst Anglo-Saxon dragons were usually located in wild, remote and ancient places – Beowulf's dragon resides in 'a steep stone burial mound high on the heath – in most surviving local legends a dragon's habitat is typically located on the borders of civilisation and their lairs close to a settlement.

Jacqueline Simpson also observes that dragon tales are 'characteristic of either coastal areas or of river valleys, and preferably of areas where hills are fairly low'. This is especially true of Yorkshire, where the majority of narratives are concentrated in the fertile, woody and relatively low-lying areas of the county, particularly Cleveland, the Vale of York and the South Yorkshire Coalfield. There are no dragons to be found in the heart of the Pennines, although what this geographical distribution says about the origin, spread and function of such legends remains unclear.

It must equally be noted that most Yorkshire dragons fail to conform to the image of a dragon as it is understood today. Although their breath is often noisome and poisonous, it is not fiery and perhaps more significantly, some examples may be described as possessing wings, but they are never reported to fly. They more typically resemble a gigantic snake – coiling up in their den and crawling along the ground, often killing their victims in the manner of a boa constrictor. Indeed, in many cases the beasts are referred to as 'worms' or 'serpents' in the original sources of the narrative.

Similarly, these monsters rarely capture or feast on young maidens as in the legend of St George and its ilk. The only place in Yorkshire with which this motif is associated is Handale. More often they simply exhibit such an insatiable appetite as to place a serious burden on the neighbouring farmers' livelihoods. Kellington's dragon devoured flocks of sheep, Wantley's stole cattle and tore up trees, whilst Sexhow's demanded the milk of nine cows daily. Meanwhile, at Filey – in one of the most original dragon legends to have emerged from Yorkshire – the dragon's unappeasable appetite is successfully used against it.

The most famous and well-developed dragon legend in Yorkshire is that of the Dragon of Wantley, and this provides a vivid retelling of the template from which all such narratives in the county (with the exception of one) seem to have been drawn. The Wantley story survives in such detail largely because it was immortalised as a popular ballad, which circulated widely as a printed broadside in the seventeenth century. The earliest surviving version comes from 1685, titled 'An Excellent Ballad of the Dreadful Combat Fought between Moore of Moore-Hall and the Dragon of Wantley' and it was subsequently included in the 1794 edition of Bishop Percy's seminal collection *Reliques of Ancient English Poetry*.

Although no such place as 'Wantley' exists in the county, the name is generally agreed to have arisen from a corruption of the village of Wortley and the nearby Wharncliffe Crags in South Yorkshire's Don Valley, a supposition supported by the ballad's correspondence with the topography of that area. The ballad relates that the dragon made its home amongst a hilltop escarpment, supposed to be Wharncliffe Crags, and from its den there ravaged the locality – devouring livestock, trees, houses and children, all whilst polluting the air with its hot, stinking breath. It often stopped at a well to drink, where it turned the water to 'burning brandy'.

The folk of the vicinity were so traumatised by the dragon's merciless assaults that they were forced to beg the aid of a 'furious knight' known as Moore of

Wharncliffe Crags above the Don Valley, once home to the famed Wantley Dragon. (Kai Roberts)

Moore-Hall. The ballad makes Moore himself sound like a scarcely less terrifying prospect than the dragon; a bawdy, hell-raising type who once in anger swung a horse by the tail and mane until it was dead, and then proceeded to eat its carcass! Still, there was probably no better hope to defeat such a beast as the dragon and Moore assented, on the sole condition that he was sent a sixteen-year-old girl to 'anoint him' overnight before the combat and dress him in the morning.

Despite his formidable strength, Moore realised that the dragon was more than an equal to him in might alone, so decided to rely on cunning to defeat it. To this end he had the steelworkers of Sheffield forge him a suit of armour covered in spikes so that the dragon could not grapple with him, and then hid in the well from which the beast was wont to drink in order to ambush it. Despite Moore's element of surprise, the two opponents were evenly matched and their struggle lasted for two days and a night, with neither receiving so much as a wound. Finally, however, Moore delivered a lucky blow to the only vulnerable spot on the dragon's body – noted in earlier, less sanitised versions of the ballad as its anus – at which the monster fell down and expired.

Whilst this ballad displays all the classic themes of a Yorkshire dragon narrative, many scholars have erroneously stated that the ballad is not an authentic local legend but actually a polemic against a historical landowner. The suggestion originates with Godfrey Bosville, a correspondent of Bishop Percy, whose theory was included as a footnote in *Reliques of Ancient English Poetry*. Bosville asserted that the ballad satirised a late sixteenth-century legal case in which Sir Francis Wortley and his tenants were embroiled over payment of tithes. According to this reading, Sir Francis is personified as the voracious dragon and Moore of Moore-Hall as the lawyer sent by the tenants to do battle with him.

Later, in his 1819 *History of Hallamshire*, the esteemed antiquarian Reverend Joseph Hunter conjectured that the ballad could refer to another dispute earlier in the sixteenth century, which arose when Sir Thomas Wortley attempted to depopulate Wharncliffe Chase to create a personal hunting ground. Yet whilst these theories have been uncritically repeated by commentators on the legend ever since, doubt was cast as early as 1864 by the local historian John Holland. Although it might be true that there was considerable antagonism between the Wortley family and their tenants during the sixteenth century, there is no evidence whatsoever to indicate that the ballad is meant to satirise these conflicts, beyond the jesting tone of the lyrics and much wishful thinking.

Considering that the story of the Dragon of Wantley is identical to a dragon-slaying narrative associated with various locations across Yorkshire (with minor local variations), it would be an insult to the skill of any balladeers to suggest that they could not have been any more inventive. It seems far more probable that this migratory legend was already attached to Wantley, along with many other sites in the county, and the composer took his inspiration from it. Whilst this does not necessarily rule out the possibility that the ballad displays satirical intent, the narrative is simply too consistent with a wider dragon-slaying tradition to suggest that it was invented solely for that purpose.

It is particularly damning to Bosville's case that the Moore family had left Moore Hall (located near Wharncliffe Crags in the Ewden Valley) half a century before the legal case the ballad is supposed to parody, and not one member of that line was ever recorded as a lawyer. Indeed, the connection between the Moore family and dragons appears to be much older than the sixteenth century. The family was associated with the area from the Norman Conquest at least and a dragon was featured on their family coat of arms. Meanwhile, there is a prominent stone effigy of a dragon in the medieval Church of St Nicholas at High Bradfield – of which the Moore family were patrons.

A dragon also features on the coat of arms of the Latimer family whose ancestral home was located at Well near Ripon, and there is a vague local legend to the effect that one of their ancestors slew such a beast at a spot between Well and Tanfield. This association between heraldry and dragons may well offer a clue as to the origin of some local dragon legends, casting them as back-formations designed to explain the choice of that particular motif in a noble family's coat of arms. Dragons were commonly employed in medieval heraldry as a symbol of power and an association with dragon-slaying was especially favoured in the fourteenth and fifteenth centuries, when the cult of St George was at its height in England.

As such, folklorists agree that a number English dragon stories represent 'charter legends' – narratives which arose to justify the origin and persistence of some social custom. In these cases, tales of dragon-slaying may have evolved to explain why a local landowning family were entitled to hold their position: namely that one of their ancestors had displayed great courage and valour in slaying a dragon which preyed on their tenants' livelihoods and children. Such a story painted the noble family as men of character, with the implication that the local community should continue to be thankful that such men had saved them from a ravening menace and remained in a position to do so again in the future, should circumstances demand it.

A similar moral can be detected in the story of Sir William Wyvill, a fourteenth-century landowner who reputedly slew a dragon that tormented the region of Slingsby in the Vale of York. However, the only narrative in which the connection between dragon-slaying and ancestral estates is made explicit is the legend of the dragon of Handale in Cleveland. This monster liked to 'beguile young damsels from the paths of truth and duty, and afterwards feed on their dainty limbs.' It was killed by a local lad called Scaw, who subsequently married an Earl's daughter he rescued from the beast's lair and thereby eventually came into possession of her father's lands. Yet, ironically, Scaw does not seem to have been an historical individual and the name may instead have been derived from a local toponym.

Nonetheless, a stone coffin supposedly belonging to Scaw was once shown in the ruins of Handale Priory and such alleged memorials are another common feature of dragon legends in Yorkshire. A similar stone coffin lid can be seen in the Church of St Edmund at Kellington, near Pontefract; it is said to commemorate Armroyd, the shepherd who with the help of his dog dispatched a sheep-killing dragon in that region. The stone appears to feature representations of a serpent and a dog, whilst a weathered carving of a cross was once thought to represent his shepherd's crook. Supposed effigies of dragon-slayers can also be seen in the churches at Slingsby and Nunnington. In both cases, the legend attached to the effigy is the same and given the geographical proximity of the two villages, it is agreed that the legends probably stem from a single source.

Effigy of Sir William Wyvill in Slingsby Church. (Kai Roberts)

The Nunnington version of the legend is given in more detail and relates that a dragon made its home on a nearby hill until it was opposed by a local knight named Sir Peter Loschy. As with Moore of Moore-Hall, Loschy was forced to rely on his cunning to defeat the beast and so he wore a suit of armour studded with razor blades so that it could not wrap itself around him and squeeze him to death like a boa constrictor. He found, however, that every time he injured the dragon, its wound immediately healed and so the battle dragged on. At length, he managed to sever part of the creature's body, whereupon his faithful dog took the piece in its jaws and carried it off to the church over a mile away. This process was repeated until the dragon was completely hacked to pieces and drew its last breath.

Although he defeated the dragon, the legend has an unhappy ending. When Sir Peter bent down to congratulate his hound, the animal licked his face and so transferred some of the dragon's poison, from which both soon expired. A tombstone in All Saints' Church at Nunnington shows the effigy of a knight resting his feet on a dog and locals have long held that this was Loschy's resting place. However, there is no record of anybody called Sir Peter Loschy being buried in the church and antiquarians have identified it as the grave of Sir Walter Leye who died in the early fourteenth century. The same story is told about a similar effigy in All Saints' Church at Slingsby, the only difference being that the identification of the tomb with Sir William Wyvill is correct. In both cases, the so-called hound at the knight's feet is more likely to be a lion – another common heraldic motif.

Such memorials are clearly a significant aspect of dragon lore in Yorkshire and nearly all examples are connected with some relic. After the milk-drinking serpent of Sexhow was slain by an anonymous knight who rode away without seeking any reward, the villagers skinned the beast and carried its pelt to the church at Stokesley, where it hung for many years. Although no such item can be seen there today, it is thought an artefact supposed to be a dragon's skin could indeed once been seen in the church. The most likely explanation, however, is that it was actually the hide of a crocodile. As the Jenny Haniver phenomenon attests, such misattributions were not uncommon amongst the uneducated in earlier centuries.

Sometimes the memorials are seen on a much larger scale in the landscape itself. This was especially true of Wharncliffe Crags: Bishop Percy recorded the testimony of a man who around 1720 had been shown the cave in which the dragon had once made its den and the well from which it drank – sites which are still marked on Ordnance Survey maps today. Meanwhile, Loschy Hill near Nunnington and Scaw Wood near Handale were supposedly named to commemorate the eponymous heroes' victories over dragons in those places. Similarly, legend maintains that a tract of land called Armroyd's Close near Kellington was given to the titular shepherd and his heirs to reward his triumph.

These are not landscape legends in the same sense as we find associated with giants or the Devil. The stories do not explain how a particular feature of the landscape came to be the way it is with reference to the activity of some supernatural or primordial being. Nor is the landscape personified as the fallen body or mark of such entities. Yet, whilst they might not be landscape legends in the truest sense, such stories nevertheless perform a similar function: connecting people to their environment through narrative. The outcome of this function is that the topographic references are then held up as proof of the legend's veracity. As Jacqueline Simpson astutely comments, these memorials represent 'a stimulus for the first invention of the legend, a focal point for its development and a memento which helps to preserve it through following generations.'

There is only one instance in Yorkshire of a landscape feature being perceived as the body of a slain dragon; namely, Filey Brigg. The legend attached to that particular locality is unique in several respects; not least in that whilst it may have originated on the Holderness coast, it was actually collected in Somerset. In narrative terms, it is the only legend in Yorkshire which does not correspond to the lone dragon-slayer model. In this case, the demise of the monster is initially an accident and the job finished off by the community as a whole. It is also more of a droll than a legend. Although it may purport to explain the origin of Filey Brigg, its primarily humorous intent is clear.

The legend tells how a tailor named Billy Biter lived in the vicinity of a dragon-haunted ravine and one misty morning tumbled over the edge into the beast's lair. Just as the dragon was about to consume this hapless individual, Billy dropped the parkin (a type of treacly gingerbread favoured in Yorkshire) he was carrying and the dragon bit down on this instead. Finding the delicacy much to its liking, the dragon spared his victim and sent him back to his cottage to fetch more. But when the henpecked Billy arrived home and told his wife the story, she refused to believe him and insisted on delivering the parkin herself.

So drunk was Billy's wife that when she reached the ravine, she too plunged over the precipice and this time, the dragon gobbled her up along with the parkin. As the dragon chewed, a morsel of the sticky cake became lodged in its teeth 'clinging so loving as an ivy-bine' and so forced the beast to attempt to wash it off in the sea. Seeing their chance, the cowed townsfolk assembled a mob with 'sledgehammers and pitchforks and axes' to prevent it returning to land. At length, a great wave came along and drowned the monster, whose bones formed the rocky reef of Filey Brigg which can be seen stretching out into the North Sea today.

Although this story was originally recorded as 'Billy Biter and the Parkin', Billy is only an inadvertent hero and a circumstantial protagonist. He may have been freed from a greedy dragon and a dipsomaniacal wife in the same day, but both his own role and the dragon-slaying are incidental to the narrative, which seems to be as much about the perils of shrewishness and the propensity of parkin to stick in one's teeth. It seems that the story was never intended to be taken seriously in the form in which it was recorded (except perhaps by children) and the existence of an alternative origin story for Filey Brigg concerning the Devil tends to support this supposition.

Nonetheless, it is an artful narrative which subverts the expectations of an audience perhaps overly familiar with tales of chivalric dragon-slayers. Billy Biter falls into the class of commoner protagonists in these legends, along with Armroyd of Kellington and Scaw of Handale, who may have gained land as a consequence of their victories, but started out as ordinary individuals. It is a notable contrast to Sir Peter Loschy, Moore of Moore Hall, Sir William Wyvill and the anonymous knight who vanquished the dragon at Sexhow. Possibly this divergent tradition arose later as a deliberate reaction to tales of the dragon-slaying gentry, offering audiences the message that they too could accomplish heroic deeds and free themselves from adversity, with the right amount of fortitude or just plain luck.

However, both these strands may ultimately have performed a similar function. As Jacqueline Simpson concludes in her study of British dragon legends:

> They foster the community's awareness of and pride in its own identity, its conviction that it is in some respect unusual, or even unique. That the lord of the manor should be descended from a dragon-slayer, that a dragon should once have roamed these very fields, or, best of all, that an ordinary lad from this very village should have outwitted and killed such a monster – these are claims to fame which any neighbouring community would be bound to envy.

Many naturalistic theories have been mooted to explain dragon legends over the years, in particular that they are allegories for some historical occurrence, such as the defeat of paganism by Christianity, conflict between the Saxons and Vikings or a simple land dispute. Yet the Victorian notion that folklore necessarily encodes and preserves the memory of ancient events and beliefs has long been doubted. Simpson's emphasis on the power they had to bind a community – both to its immediate topographic environment and to its social institutions – seems a far less fanciful account of their evolution.

Complete with their medieval tombstones and heraldic associations, Yorkshire dragons probably emerged from the conditions of the late Middle Ages, when new communities and social institutions were being forged and stabilised. Like so many motifs in English folklore, the dragon represented an outside threat to the stability of those communities and institutions, a destructive force beyond their control which must be overcome through virtues such as selflessness and courage if the community wished to survive. The threat of the hostile 'other' is still exploited today for such purposes, and whilst these outsiders may be portrayed more subtly than a dragon, they are often every bit as imaginary.

FOUR

GIANTS

In English legend, there are typically two categories of giant: the landscape-shaping oaf and the murderous ogre. Neither type is particularly intelligent; whether they are engaged in terrorising local villages or some colossal construction, their schemes are often characterised by clumsiness and stupidity. As a result, it can seem that by the time they were first recorded, such legends were not taken very seriously. Perhaps they were told as drolls for the benefit of credulous travellers or bedtime stories with which to subdue unruly children. However, these roles are often the final function of narratives that once had a more serious purpose, and beneath the whimsical veneer, they often have much to tell us about the way past generations perceived the world in which they lived.

To deal first with the landscape-shaping variety of giant, it is no surprise to find that Yorkshire is fertile territory for these legends, especially in the north and west ridings. Distinctive landscape features invariably accrue an enduring glut of folklore and the uplands of the Pennines or North York Moors bristle with such vistas. Characteristically, these tales purport to account for the origin of certain topographic prominences and it may well be that these narratives were the sincere product of the pre-modern mind's tendency to anthropomorphise its environment. Long before even the most basic principles of geology had taken hold in the popular psyche, the grit stone crags and ancient megaliths which strew the Yorkshire countryside must have seemed the work of some titanic race that stalked the land in days gone by.

Quite how long these legends may have survived before the advent of modernity is uncertain. Giants appear in the creation mythologies of a great number of pre-modern cultures – including those of early settlers of the British Isles such as the

Celts, the Saxons and the Norse – and they still inspired belief by the late Middle Ages. Geoffrey of Monmouth claimed that giants were the original occupants of Britain in his influential twelfth-century tome, *The History of the Kings of Britain*, as did Raphael Holinshead in his *Chronicles of England, Scotland and Ireland*, written as late as 1587. When even educated men expressed such ideas, it is scarcely surprising that giants persisted so stubbornly in the minds of the general populace and the annals of local legend.

Perhaps more than any other traditional folk narrative, giant lore expresses what Anthony Roberts, a previous writer on these myths, calls 'the topography of legend': giants not only dwelled in these locations, they *formed* them. As such, we may also consider that even as this belief ebbed away and the legends were no longer accepted literally, the storytelling tradition ensured that tales of landscape-shaping giants continued to relate man to his immediate environment. The local farmer might not have genuinely believed that a giant once fashioned the hillside on which he grazed his flocks, but the stories he had heard growing up still invested that landscape with colour and significance. He may equally have felt pride that such a narrative was attached to *his* neighbourhood, with the giant becoming a sort of local mascot. It is a function that endures in tourist-lore today.

Moreover, before man was readily able to shape his own environment through the advancement of technology, giants were a particularly apposite metaphor for his place in the world. As the psychologist Brian Bates writes in relation to how giants were perceived by our Anglo-Saxon and Norse ancestors, 'Cleverer beings may have come along since and elaborated the world but the basic structure and dynamics of life were in the hands of the giants … The giants reminded them that human life existed within a universe of immense forces.' Essentially this remained true until the Industrial Revolution and just as the upland fastnesses of Yorkshire responded well to particularly austere forms of Christianity such as Methodism, they similarly identified with the giants' embodiment of the brute reality of nature.

Like the changeable elements of the Pennine hills, giants were quick to anger and the summits and valleys of that range exhibit the consequences of their temper. Anomalous stone boulders or outcrops were often attributed to the work of giants, flung from an eminence nearby and often they were in fact glacial erratics, carried and deposited from some hilltop strata by retreating ice-sheets several millennia ago. Such a rock once sat about a mile from Leeds, beside the Bradford road. It was known as the Giant's Stone and local legend related that it had been thrown there from a hill near Armley on the opposite bank of the River Aire. Indentations on the boulder were imagined to represent the giant's fingerprints.

Meanwhile, the Carlow Stone was supposedly thrown by a giant from the summit of Addleborough in Wensleydale. He was aiming at his adversary the Devil, who had taken up a position on a hilltop across the valley, but his pitch fell short and it came to rest on the shores of Semer Water below. A similar story is told about the creation of Almscliffe Crag, a substantial gritstone excrescence that sits several hundred feet

The Cow and Calf on Ilkley Moor, stepping stones of the giant Rombald. (Kai Roberts)

above lower Wharfedale and provides a focal point from miles around. In this case, the Devil and the giant, Rombald were fighting on Ilkley Moor when the Devil overshot and his missile landed some eight miles away to form Almscliffe Crag.

Rombald is the tutelary giant of that region and supposedly gave his name to Rombald's Moor – the upland massif between Airedale and Wharfedale, of which Ilkley Moor forms the northern edge. In some versions of the legend, the stray missile which formed Almscliffe Crag was thrown at Rombald not by the Devil but by the giant's formidable wife. Rombald himself is supposed to be responsible for the natural basins which score the surface of the Crag, which he created when he strode across to Almscliffe from his home above Ilkley and left his footprints embedded in the rock. On another occasion when the giant was stepping between these two points, he missed his footing and gouged a mark in face of the Cow, largest of the famed Cow and Calf Rocks – a favourite recreation spot for locals and day-trippers alike for many centuries.

Rombald's wife was also credited with the Hitching Stone, a huge boulder on Keighley Moor above Cowling, reckoned to be one of the largest single pieces of rock in the entire county. This monolith is further distinguished by a tubular cavity which runs for 20 feet through the rock at an angle of forty-five degrees from the top of the stone to a substantial recess on the west rock-face, known as the Druid's Chair. Geologists believe this feature was formed by a fossilised tree which once ran through the boulder but has since corroded away. Local folklore, however, claims that the cavity is the result of the female giant driving a broom handle into the stone and flinging it over her head from Rombald's Moor!

As Yorkshire giants go, the fame of Rombald and his wife was matched only by that of Wade and his clan, who occupied the North York Moors around Eskdale and indulged in similar behaviour. Legend records that Wade had a wife named Bel and a proportionally gigantic infant son. One day, the child had been left to his own devices whilst Bel milked her herd of cows on Swarth Howe above Aislaby, but growing impatient for attention, he took a huge rock and hurled it at his mother. For once in such a story, the giant's aim was true and it struck Bel with enough force to send her flying to the ground where she left the imprint of her form in the rocks. Sadly, the stone that supposedly bore the impression of the giantess has long since been quarried away.

Sometimes giants not only leave their mark on the landscape, but become personified in the landscape itself. A nearly forgotten tale from West Yorkshire relates that a tribe of giants once dwelled in Magdale near Huddersfield. When a daughter of this tribe went missing, her frantic father scoured the surrounding countryside until he heard that she had last been seen on the hills above Holmfirth. The giant leapt from Scar Top at Netherton with such force that he left his footprint embedded in a stone there, and landed at Wolfstones Height, where he found his daughter's prostrate form. At first he thought she was merely sleeping, but as he drew closer he saw that she had succumbed to exposure and died. He left her in that place to rest, which is why the summit of Wolfstones Height forms the simulacrum of a recumbent child and is known locally as the Child o'th'Edge.

Another West Yorkshire legend recalls a more solitary and rather less tender giant, who made his home on the moors above Haworth and quickly became the scourge of the district. To sate his considerable appetites he would steal the livestock from local farms and valuables from travellers on the road across the tops. For many years, his neighbours turned a blind eye to the giant's behaviour, as they were afraid to confront such a terrible monster. However, during one particularly harsh winter when food was scarce, the giant began to eat people. At this point, the local folk finally decided that they could tolerate no more and they formed a mob to drive their tormentor out.

Like many of his race when confronted with an equal adversary, the giant proved to be a coward. He saw the mob coming and tried to flee, but they pursued their quarry at length and caught the brute at the Forks House stile. Their numbers were such that they were able to easily overcome the giant and decapitated him, allowing his head to roll into the delph below. His body, meanwhile, turned to stone and it is said that a fragment of the giant's petrified form can still be seen beside the path which leads from the Brontë waterfalls to Top Withins. This relic is known as the Cuckoo Stone, although authorities are divided as to whether it is actually a natural earth-fast rock or an artificial standing stone.

If the Cuckoo Stone was an ancient standing stone, this would be entirely consistent with other giant lore, as local legend is just as ready to attribute the anomaly of ancient megaliths to the work of giants. A substantial Bronze-Age burial

Little Skirtful of Stones on Rombald's Moor, spilled by the giant's wife. (Kai Roberts)

cairn on Burley Moor (part of the Rombald's Moor massif) known as Little Skirtful of Stones was variously credited to Rombald or his wife. In one version of the tale, his wife spilled the stones she was carrying in her apron whilst stalking across the moor in pursuit of her husband. In another, the stones were dropped by Rombald himself as he carried them to construct a bridge over the River Wharfe in the valley below. Similar tales are told of the creation of the less well-preserved Great Skirtful of Stones nearby, although some sources suggest this cairn in fact marked the grave of the giant.

The motif of a giant's grave was frequently attached to actual ancient burial sites, suggesting that folk may have dimly recognised the purpose of such monuments long before barrow-digging antiquarians confirmed it. The substantial dimensions of such tombs must have seemed fit for giants and there are a number of places known as 'Giant's Grave' spread across the county. Although many lack any detailed narrative, their names remain as a clue to the associated lore. Sadly, a number have been entirely destroyed by deep-soil ploughing and stone theft over the centuries, but a particularly notable example can still be seen in Halton Gill, beneath the distinctive bulk of Pen-y-ghent. The badly damaged site remains largely inscrutable, but it is thought to represent the remains of a late Neolithic chambered cairn or an early Bronze Age round barrow.

The remains of the chambered cairn known as Stony Raise on the flanks of Addleborough in Wensleydale represent the largest example of such a monument

Wade's Stone near East Barnby, grave marker of the legendary giant. (Kai Roberts)

in Yorkshire, even after a great quantity of stone was removed for building material in the early nineteenth century. It is scarcely surprising that such an imposing site became associated with the activity of giants. The cairn was supposedly created when a giant transported a heavy chest of gold from Skipton Castle to Pendragon Castle in the Eden Valley. As he crossed Addleborough, the burden became too great and he collapsed, letting the horde fall to the ground beside him. This accident caused the giant to blaspheme and at this exhortation the earth itself rose over the chest in pious defiance.

Meanwhile, Wade was supposedly buried beneath a standing stone known as Wade's Stone or Wade's Grave, near East Barnby. There was once a second stone some 12 feet away from the first and it was believed that these two marked his head and feet respectively. This site stands a small distance from the shell of Mulgrave Castle, also reputedly the work of Wade. The ruins seen today are actually the remains of the second castle to have stood on the site, constructed in the late eleventh century by Nigel Fossard, who was gifted land around Whitby by the Conqueror himself, and not destroyed until 1647 on the orders of the Long Parliament, following its use as a Royalist garrison during the Civil Wars.

However, the Norman castle replaced an earlier Saxon fortification and it was this building which was credited to Wade. In this version of Wade's legend, he was Duke Wada, a Saxon noble and one of the conspirators who murdered Ethelred, King of Northumberland, around AD 849-862. The story was first recorded by

William Camden in his seminal antiquarian work, *Britannia*, published between 1586 and 1607. He also notes that, 'Here within the hill between two entire and solid stones above seven foot high (Wada) lies entombed: which stones because they stand eleven foot asunder, the people doubt not to affirm that he was a might giant.' Nonetheless, there is no corroborative evidence for Camden's Duke Wada, so it seems probable that this is a back-formation and the legend of the giant Wade circulated in these parts long before the name of the Saxon duke.

Local legend also relates that Wade built Mulgrave Castle at the same time as his wife Bel was building Pickering Castle, but having only one hammer between them, they would regularly throw it to each other across the moors. To facilitate their movement across this hilly terrain, the giants were supposed to have constructed Wade's Causeway – actually a well-preserved Roman road running from Eskdale to Malton across Wheeldale Moor. Legend claims Bel used this road to access her herd of cattle for milking. The giantess seems to have been particularly associated with her cattle and during the eighteenth century, credulous visitors to Mulgrave Castle were shown the jawbone of a whale and told it was the rib of one of Bel's cows.

It seems entirely plausible that prior to the growth of antiquarianism in the sixteenth and seventeenth centuries, the general populace sincerely believed that only giants could have been responsible for edifices such as prehistoric megaliths and Roman roads. Long after the knowledge of their construction was lost, these remarkable feats of engineering must have seemed beyond the capabilities of any normal-sized human. One writer on giant lore, H.J. Massingham, suggests this process may have actually started in the prehistoric period itself as the non-megalith building Celts of the Iron Age looked back on the work of the Neolithic and Bronze Age Britons with wonder and bafflement. Of course, it is a theory that is entirely impossible to verify.

Still, many commentators have regarded landscape-shaping giants as a direct inheritance from pagan belief, perhaps a corrupted remembrance of pre-Christian creation deities. This may possibly be true in the case of Wade, who seems to have been derived from a character common to Norse and Germanic mythology. The earliest reference to this figure is found in an eighth-century Anglo-Saxon poem called 'Widsith', although the majority of what is actually known about him comes from the 'Saga of Thidrek of Bern', which only survives as a thirteenth-century fragment. In these sources, he is a sea-dwelling giant who ascends to dwell on land and father the more famous Wayland the Smith.

However, by the late medieval period, the giant Wade seems to have been remembered in England not as a mythological demi-god, but a heroic warrior. Most of the stories attached to his name have been lost, although one is preserved in Walter Map's twelfth-century work, 'De Nugis Curilaium', in which Wade is portrayed as a comrade of the eighth-century Mercian king, Offa, and together they repel a Roman invasion (despite the fact that by that time, Rome had long since lost interest in Britain). Otherwise, Wade only receives passing mentions in Geoffrey Chaucer's fourteenth-century poems, *The Canterbury Tales* and *Troilus and Criseyde*, and Thomas Mallory's fifteenth-century compilation of Arthurian legends, *Le Morte d'Arthur*.

Wade's legend seems mostly to have died out with the Middle Ages in England, other than in the stories told around the North York Moors. Nonetheless, it seems unlikely that his persistence in the region represents evidence of an enduring Norse pagan heritage. These stories of Wade bear far more resemblance to the sort of narrative commonly found associated with other medieval heroes such as King Arthur and Robin Hood, who in local legend are often transformed into giants. As Katharine Briggs notes, 'Often monstrous traits are attached to heroes, who sometimes seem to have changed from gods to heroes and from heroes to giants.' Such similarities make it seem more probable that Wade's North Yorkshire legend was a distortion of the popular medieval hero rather than a relic of the mythological figure.

It is often the case that giant legends derive not from the Viking occupation of northern England or earlier, as was commonly assumed by early folklorists, but from the medieval period. Giants were a popular civic mascot during the Middle Ages – possibly following their role in Geoffrey of Monmouth's 'History of the Kings of Britain' – and were frequently represented in architecture and their effigies displayed during pageants. Thus, Rombald was probably not a remembrance of the Old Norse giant 'Raumr' (meaning 'big and ugly') as some have suggested, but a corruption of Robert de Romille, the first Norman Lord of Skipton. Romille perhaps gave his name to the moor during his tenure and the legend of the giant Rombald was a back-formation created to account for the title long after its true origin had been forgotten by the local populace.

Another Yorkshire giant for whom a Norse origin has been suggested is the savage resident of Penhill in Wensleydale, whose legend is one of the most developed in the county. According to the story, this giant once owned all the land around Penhill which he used to graze his swine – the largest herd in Yorkshire and the giant's primary source of his wealth. He took great pride in this asset and frequently spent his time riding amongst his swine, counting their number and rounding them up with his loyal hound, Wolfhead. However, the giant showed no fondness towards any humans in the neighbourhood and he was a great source of terror to them, often taking pleasure in letting Wolfhead harry their flocks.

One day he was indulging in this cruel pastime, he encountered a young shepherdess named Gunda, who implored him to desist before he destroyed the flock and ruined her family. At first the giant merely laughed at her pleas, but after a while he began to notice how attractive this girl was and started to make advances towards her. Profoundly discomfited by this attention, Gunda fled, but this only made the giant more determined and he congratulated himself on having found such a pretty quarry to hunt. Of course, the girl's speed was no match for Wolfhead

Penhill rising above Wensleydale, home of a legendary giant. (Phil Roper)

and the hound eventually brought her down. As he did so, however, Gunda managed to lay her hands on a large rock and struck out at the beast, causing it to yelp and slink back to its master. This action so angered the giant that he strode forward and with a single blow from his spiked club, slew the girl as she lay helpless.

As news of his deed spread through the district, resentment towards the giant began to fester even further and sometime later, as he was riding amongst his herd, the giant noticed that one of his precious swine was missing. Up until this point, Wolfhead had been his only living friend, but with this discovery, the giant turned on his faithful dog, roundly abusing it for its failure to protect his property. With a vicious kick, he sent the hound out to search for the missing animal but thereafter it would not return to his calls. Instead, it sat on the edge of the woods, just out of range of the giant's missiles and howled plaintively in the direction of the castle.

At length, the giant himself discovered the lost boar, pierced by an arrow and lying dead in the undergrowth. He was so incensed by this outrage that he demanded every man and boy in the neighbourhood capable of wielding a bow assemble outside his castle. The giant ordered them to give up the person responsible for killing the swine but when nobody came forward, he told them that they must assemble there again at sunset the following day along with their wives and children, and if he still did not have the culprit, he would kill the lastborn male of every family. Upon hearing this threat, an old man known as the Seer of Carperby stepped forward from the crowd and warned the giant that if he left the castle tomorrow with evil in his heart, he would never again enter its walls – alive or dead.

The giant initially laughed off this prophecy but he was secretly perturbed. When morning came the next day, one of his few loyal retainers told the giant that he'd dreamt nine ravens had circled the castle and alighted on its battlements before cawing nine times. The ancient retainer thought it must surely be an evil omen and advised the giant not to follow through with his threat to the local children. However, this infuriated the giant who beat his old servant for daring to voice such dark thoughts and then left the castle intent on brutalising his neighbours into submission. After the giant had left, the bleeding and resentful retainer summoned his remaining strength, gathered together all the peat, straw and furniture he could find in the castle and built it into a great pyre.

Meanwhile, as the giant progressed towards the spot where the local villagers were assembled, he discovered another nine of his boar felled with arrows. This drove the giant into a bloodthirsty rage and he swore that unless those responsible came forward, he would slaughter every man, woman and child right there on the hillside. But as he ranted, the Seer of Carperby pointed to the plume of black smoke now rising from the giant's castle. Observing that the prophecy had come true, the giant was aghast but as he turned to slay the Seer, an even more unnerving sight met his eyes. Before him stood the apparition of the shepherdess he had so callously murdered, holding Wolfhead on a leash. The giant stepped back in horror as Gunda released the hound and it leapt at its former master's throat, so driving the tyrant over the edge of a nearby cliff to his death.

Much has been claimed for the legend of the giant of Penhill. Its collector, Richard Fairfax-Blakeborough, believed it to be descended from 'the sagas of the Norsemen', whilst a later commentator thought it represented evidence of a lost chalk hill-figure created during the Bronze Age. However, neither of these hypotheses seem to be supported by the narrative itself: the tale has little in common with the Norse sagas and it is certainly unlikely to be as old as the Bronze Age. Rather, the story appears to preserve a distorted memory of a cruel local landowner, possibly an early Norman lord who was excessively harsh in his prosecution of forest law in the Forest of Wensleydale. Under such law, an offender could be executed for killing any game animal (such as a boar) and it was so deeply unpopular that veiled criticisms survive in many medieval texts.

The giant of Penhill falls into the second category of giant found in English folklore: the murderous ogre. Many of these legends display characteristics which suggest they derive from the medieval period. Indeed, a few seem to have been created to stress the knightly credentials of local landowning families and in this respect have a great deal in common with many dragon legends (See Chapter Three). These stories even have similar legendary relics in church architecture. For instance, in the All Saints' Church at Wighill near Tadcaster there is a tomb which bears the effigy of a knight and on one side, the grotesque carving of a head.

Although the monument is no older than the seventeenth century, local legend has interpreted it as the burial place of a famed giant-killer – the carved head on its side representing that of the monster he slew.

The legend describes how the district was being terrorised by a giant of Turkish origin who lived on a small island off the coast and came ashore to feast on children. Such was the giant's notoriety, a reward for its execution was offered by the king himself. Nobody dared take up the challenge but a young lad named Stapleton, who sailed out to the island and confronted the monster. After a lengthy struggle, the giant succeeded in knocking Stapleton to the ground, but as it moved to deliver a final blow, the boy thrust his sword through his adversary's armpit and so mortally wounded the brute. He finished the job by decapitating the giant and carrying its head back to the king as evidence of his victory. Stapleton was rewarded with the Manor of Wighill, which his family owned for many generations thereafter.

A legend attached to Sessay in the Vale of York seems to have performed a similar function, explaining how a particular family came to own land in that district. Thomas Parkinson gives a particularly vivid description of the giant that once plagued the people thereabouts:

> He was a huge brute in human form – legs like elephants' legs, arms of a corresponding size, a face most fierce to look upon with only one eye placed in the midst of his forehead; a mouth large as a lion's and garnished with teeth as long as the prongs of a hayfork. His only clothing was a cow's hide fastened across his breast, and with the hair outwards; while over his shoulders he usually carried a stout young tree, as a club for offence and defence. Now and then he made the woods ring with demoniacal laughter; now and then with savage, unearthly growls.

The villagers attempted to band together to drive their tormentor out, but invariably lost their resolve at the last moment. It was not until Sir Guy D'Aunay of Cowick Castle in South Yorkshire came to Sessay that the giant finally met its match. He had come to visit Joan Darrell, daughter of an old friend of his father's, to ask for the girl's hand in marriage and admitted that this was primarily in the interests of a union of their families' estates. Miss Darrell admired Sir Guy's honesty and being a canny individual, replied that if the knight could slay the giant that so persecuted her tenants and left her servants unwilling to enter the wood to collect kindling, then she would assent to his request.

In addition to its taste for small children and local farmers' livestock, the giant liked to steal sacks of meal from the local windmill which it used to mix with the blood of slaughtered animals to create a grisly porridge. Hearing of this, Sir Guy staked out the mill and sure enough after a while, the giant came along. Made wary by the size of the ogre, the knight bided his time, spying on his quarry from the trees. His caution was soon rewarded for as the giant reached through an upper window of the building to snatch a sack, the wind changed direction and one of the sails of the mill struck it on the head, sending the colossus sprawling to the ground. Seizing the opportunity, Sir Guy ran over and drove his sword through the giant's single eye. His marriage to Joan Darrell followed shortly afterwards and the D'Aunay family came into possession of her Sessay estates.

A very similar legend is attached to the village of Dalton nearby, and the parallels are so pronounced, it seems that the two tales must stem from the same source. However, whilst the Sessay narrative is a typical medieval charter-legend, the Dalton story is inverted, with a commoner as the hero and may well have represented the vernacular form of Sessay's gentrified myth. Dalton's giant was similarly cyclopic and a mill also features in the legend. But whereas the Sessay giant stole from the local mill, the Dalton giant resides in one and uses it to grind meal from human bones to bake into bread. It spared only one victim from this fate: a young boy who was captured on Pilmoor and kept as a servant to help with the milling.

Unsurprisingly, the boy resented his confinement and one day asked permission to visit the celebrated Topcliffe Fair. When the giant refused, the boy decided that he would take his leave anyway. He waited until the giant had gorged himself and fallen into a slumber, took the knife it had used to cut bread and like Sir Guy D'Aunay stabbed directly into the monster's eye. Unfortunately, this did not kill the giant straight away and the brute rose up, blocking the only door. But the boy still had a trick up his sleeve and as the giant raged, he killed and then skinned his master's dog. Draping the pelt over his shoulders, the boy dropped down onto all fours and began to bark. Unable to tell the difference, the half-blind giant let the boy crawl through his legs to the door and safety.

The giant must have succumbed to his wound eventually, as a tumulus known as Giant's Grave once stood beside the mill at Dalton – although it had long since been destroyed by the time the legend was recorded in the late nineteenth century. Whilst this has something in common with the tradition of landscape-shaping giants, the Dalton example is in all other respects a typical ogre, much like the giants of Wighill and Sessay. It is possible that these three represent a corrupted memory of some brutal outlaw leader, but they are all conceived as a classic bogeyman figure and by the time these legends were recorded, they were probably told only as bedtime stories to children or to tease gullible visitors.

This certainly seems to be the case with the giant that occupied Yordas Cave in Kingsdale. Although this cavern is now accessible to anyone with a sturdy pair of boots and the spirit of adventure, during the nineteenth century it was a show-cave, with a fee charged for guided tours. One sightseer records being shown, 'the great hall of Yordas – the fabulous giant from Norway – and there we see his throne, his bed-chamber, his fitch of bacon, his mill and his oven, wherein he ground and baked the big white stones or the bones of naughty boys and girls into bread.' However, it is unclear if this is anything more than an invention of the tour-guide. There is no Nordic giant named Yordas and the name more likely derives from the Old Norse phrase *jord ass* meaning 'earth stream' – doubtless a reference to the subterranean waterfall which dominates the main chamber.

Nonetheless, this evolution (or devolution?) is a familiar folkloric process and the transition of narratives from sincere belief, to fireside yarn, to children's story is widely recognised. Whilst it now seems excessive to claim that legends encode the beliefs of pre-Christian cultures – as many early folklorists did – a kernel of historic conviction may still be found in many of these narratives. Whether that is the animistic personification of prominent landscape features, an incredulity at the size of prehistoric megaliths or the memory of some feared local tyrant, the stories provide a valuable glimpse into the concerns and cosmologies of the people who first told them and the generations that preserved them.

FIVE
FAIRY LORE

In the summer of 1917, ten-year-old Frances Griffiths and her sixteen-year-old cousin Elsie Wright claimed to have captured two photographs of fairies playing around Cottingley Beck, near Bradford. By 1920, news of these remarkable images had reached the creator of Sherlock Holmes and prominent Spiritualist, Sir Arthur Conan Doyle, who was working on an article about fairies for the Christmas edition of *The Strand Magazine*. At their request, the two girls produced another three photographs and all five pictures were unleashed upon the general public over the following year to a considerable storm of publicity. Although very few commentators were as credulous as Doyle, the story nonetheless provided a popular talking point and gripped the British imagination for many decades thereafter.

In 1983, improved photographic analysis techniques finally pushed the cousins into admitting that they had faked the photographs, using cardboard figures copied from a popular children's book of the era. Whilst a study of folklore is not the place to examine the historical and philosophical dynamics that led to the hoax being so readily accepted by Doyle and his ilk, or the public sensation that followed, the episode can nonetheless be seen as a manifestation of a centuries-old fairy tradition in Yorkshire, a tradition in which Frances Griffiths and Elsie Wright had once been thoroughly initiated. For although Elsie disavowed all the photographs, Frances continued to maintain that the fifth and final image was genuine, and both women insisted until their dying day that they really had seen fairies around Cottingley Beck.

In the previous century, a number of striking accounts of fairy sightings were recorded in the region, often purporting to be the personal experiences of respectable, upstanding citizens whose word could not be questioned. In the mid-1800s, for instance, a labourer named Henry Roundell was known to have encountered fairies early one morning somewhere in Washburndale, possibly in the vicinity of Fewston. When the report was published in 1870, the journalist's correspondent saw fit to note, 'A shrewd fellow he was, who knew quite well the difference between a pound and a shilling: and a steady church-goer … If he had not been such an exceedingly respectable man, all would have been set down at once to a mere drunkard's fancy.'

Roundell claimed that after rising unusually early one morning, he had set off to hoe a field of turnips and upon arriving at his destination a little before sunrise, noticed that the leaves seemed to be:

> … stirring strangely. When he looked again he saw that what was moving about were not turnip-leaves at all. Between every row of them was a row of little men, all dressed in green, and all with tiny hoes in their hands. They were hoeing away with might and main; and chattering and singing to themselves meanwhile, but in an odd, shrill, cracked voice, like a lot of field-crickets. They had hats on their heads, something in the shape of foxglove bells, Roundell thought, but he was not near enough to distinguish them plainly, only he was quite certain they were all dressed in green, the same colour as the turnip leaves.

Up until this point, the story is in many ways atypical. It is quite unusual to find fairies engaged in any form of labour; often they are portrayed as decadent, hedonistic beings forever revelling in the moonlight and dependent on pilfering the fruits of human endeavour for the necessities of life. However, it concludes as so many fairy narratives do. Roundell proceeded to stumble over the gate to the field and alert the field's occupants to his presence, whereupon they all immediately fled: 'Whirr! Whirr! off went the little men like innumerable coveys of partridge.' If there is any recurrent theme to narratives concerning the fairies, it is that they are shy creatures who resent humans spying or interfering in their affairs.

Yorkshire is the scene of one of the earliest recorded fairy narratives in England and even several hundred years prior to Roundell's experience, these creatures were portrayed as profoundly hostile to uninvited human intrusion. The legend was documented around 1198 by the monk, William of Newburgh, who wrote that he had known it since his childhood, suggesting an even older provenance. Indeed, it is one of the most common migratory legends in English fairy lore and a version was recorded in Gloucestershire only thirty years later. Although William does not explicitly identify the location of this fairy encounter, it is clearly supposed to be Willy Howe, a Bronze Age burial mound on the Yorkshire Wolds, close by that

Willy Howe, a Bronze Age tumulus on the Yorkshire Wolds haunted by fairies. (Kai Roberts)

mysterious stream, the Gypsey Race. The theme of hollow hills and prehistoric burial sites is a common one in fairy lore.

In William's account, a peasant returning home late at night was disturbed by the sound of singing and feasting emerging from Willy Howe as he rode past. Deciding to investigate further, he discovered a door into the barrow and beyond this portal, 'a large and luminous house, full of people, who were reclining as at a solemn banquet'. As the peasant entered, an attendant offered him a cup, but rather than drink from it, he poured out the contents and tried to pocket the vessel. Unfortunately, the fairies noticed his actions and 'great tumult arose at the banquet'. The assembled host then pursued him as he fled from the barrow and he was only able to escape thanks to the swiftness of his horse. However, the adventure had been worth it. The purloined cup proved to be fashioned from an unknown material and of such rare quality that he later presented it to King Henry I.

Perhaps it is unwise to assume that the fairies seen by Henry Roundell and William of Newburgh's rustic were the same category of being. Folklorist Jeremy Harte has observed that during the medieval period, they were typically referred to as elves and the idea of a universal class of 'fairies' did not emerge in popular tradition until much later. The term 'fairy' has an Old French root and whilst it was a popular term in late medieval romances, primarily consumed by a courtly audience, the word does not seem to have appeared in vernacular English until the eighteenth century. It was only following this that fairies in native folklore began to assume the characteristics which we typically ascribe to them today. For instance, diminutive size was not a characteristic of any fairy-type entity until the Victorian period; it is instructive that whilst Roundell describes the fairies he saw as 'tiny', William of Newburgh makes no such reference.

It may be, therefore, that during the nineteenth century a number of diverse entities were subsumed under the catch-all term 'fairy', distorting their original significance. Given the passion of Victorian collectors for taxonomising, this would hardly be surprising. One feature common to fairy lore of all ages, however, seems to be the idea of a parallel society to our own, but one that is largely invisible to us and sometimes antagonistic. Indeed, the seventeenth-century Scottish minister, Reverend Robert Kirk, dubbed it 'The Secret Commonwealth'. This society also seems to have been more intimately connected to the natural world than our own and it is significant that whilst ideas about fairy physiognomy and behaviour changed over the centuries, the places they were supposed to inhabit remained more constant – in the northern counties at least.

Thus, when Thomas Wright visited Willy Howe around 1861, he discovered that the twelfth-century legend was still well known in the locality. Assuming that Victorian farmers on the Wolds were not familiar with the work of medieval chroniclers, the narrative had survived almost 700 years through oral transmission alone – although the tale told to Wright had a slightly different twist to the conclusion. In that version, when the vessel was offered to the peasant at the banquet, it appeared to be made from pure silver; yet when he got it home, he discovered that it was nothing more than base metal and mostly worthless. Wright also notes that few locals would pass Willy Howe after dark and were greatly concerned when some antiquarians had previously attempted to excavate the barrow, fearing the supernatural retribution that might follow.

Another story about Willy Howe was recorded by William Hone in his *Table Book* of 1827. In this story, a fairy maiden was uncharacteristically smitten with a local man and she told him that if he visited the top of the barrow every morning, he would find a guinea coin awaiting him. She only warned him not to inform anybody else. At first, the man heeded the injunction and he always attended the spot alone, each time finding his guinea reward as promised. But clearly this secret knowledge was too great for him to bear alone and eventually he invited a friend to accompany him to the top of the Howe. Following this, not only did the gift of guineas cease, but 'he met with a severe punishment from the fairies for his presumption'. Sadly, Hone does not record the exact nature of the retribution meted out.

Some idea of fairy justice can be ascertained from other stories, however. For instance, an Eskdale farmer got more than he bargained for when he accepted a wager to enter Mulgrave Woods late one night and call out Jeanie of Biggersdale, an infamously ill-tempered fairy who lived at the head of that dell. Emboldened by alcohol, the farmer approached her dwelling and called her name; unfortunately for him, Jeanie was at home and at once replied that she was coming, her voice ripe with fury. The farmer turned heel and fled, with the irate fairy in hot pursuit. He managed to escape by crossing the running stream – a boundary which no denizen of the Otherworld can traverse – but Jeanie was so nearly upon him that she managed to snatch at the rear half of his horse before the animal was fully across and her supernatural touch severed the animal in two.

Others only happened to provoke the fairies' wrath by accident or momentary indiscretion. Those who had the misfortune to stumble upon the nocturnal fairy revels at Gilstead Crag, for example, would immediately be deprived of their sight. Similarly, when a native of Threshfield in Wharfedale was staggering home drunk one night, his route took him by Elbolton Hill – a notorious haunt of the fairy folk. Sure enough, their festivities were in full swing and the inebriate's sense proved so befuddled that he unwisely attempted to accompany them with a song. Instantly, the party rounded on the interloper, tormenting him with pinches and kicks until he finally managed to escape. In the melee, however, he succeeded in pocketing one of the tiny beings, and thought to present it to his daughters as a living doll. But when he arrived home, not a trace of the fairy was to be found.

Elbolton's association with fairies was very strong in Wharfedale folklore and this is hardly surprising as the hill possesses at least three features which are frequently identified as marks of fairy habitation. Elbolton is one of the Cracoe Reef Knolls, distinctively shaped hills formed from the remnants of a prehistoric coral reef many millions of years ago. As such, its profile is classically dome-shaped and whilst it is not particularly high at little more than 1,000 feet, it is topographically prominent. Hills of this nature are often identified with fairies; for instance, Schiehallion in Perthshire, otherwise known as the Fairy Hill of the Caledonians; or Doon Hill in Stirlingshire, which was identified as a fairy haunt by Reverend Robert Kirk in his famous tome of 1691, *The Secret Commonwealth of Elves, Fauns and Fairies*.

Elbolton's unique limestone geology also means that it is riddled with potholes and the fairies' connection with subterranean, chthonic spaces is also firmly

Elbolton Hill in Wharfedale, notorious haunt of the fairies. (Kai Roberts)

established. Similar examples in Yorkshire include the Fairy Parlour, a natural fissure which leads some hundred yards into the famed millstone grit outcrop of Almscliffe Crag. It is said that when some brave cavers attempted to explore this passage sometime in the nineteenth century, they were forced to retreat by the sound of the belligerent fairies rattling their shovels and pokers within. Several miles away in Lady Wood near Collingham, there was also a cave called the Fairy Hole from which locals claimed the sound of fairy revels could often be heard.

However, Elbolton's most significant association is with the remains of our prehistoric ancestors. During excavation of an Elbolton cave known as Navvy Noddle Hole in 1888, the remains of twelve Neolithic humans were discovered, along with a quantity of Neolithic and Bronze-Age pottery and the bones of long-extinct animals. The link between fairies and the Bronze-Age burial mound, Willy Howe, has already been discussed, whilst Pudding Pie Hill near Thirsk represents another example. Originally a Bronze-Age barrow, this site was reused by Anglo-Saxon settlers in the Dark Ages and excavation revealed several burials, accompanied by rich grave goods. Significantly, local folklore had long claimed that if a person ran round the barrow nine times and stuck a knife in the top, they would be able to hear the fairies babbling within.

This relationship between ancient burial sites and the fairies is repeated across the British Isles, and it may be relevant that in some northern traditions, the fairies are regarded as the spirits of the unbaptised, pre-Christian dead. Some folklorists have even suggested that oral transmission of fairy legends preserved a corrupted memory of barrows and so forth as burial grounds, long after their actual history had been forgotten. A similar (albeit largely discredited) theory holds that the fairies originated as an ancient folk-memory of conquered races who took refuge in rock-shelters and caves during the waves of prehistoric migration and invasion. This hypothesis ably explains the fairies' connection with rocky and subterranean places, but such a reductive rationalisation cannot do justice to the diversity and dynamism of the fairy tradition through the ages.

It may simply be that fairy locations were classically liminal and so inevitably became associated with the supernatural in the pre-modern psyche. Such symbolism seems to be an intrinsic feature of the collective consciousness which manifests in diverse cultures across time and space. This would account for the fact that fairies are also similarly associated with water sources. The Queen of the Craven fairies was believed to dwell behind the picturesque waterfall of Jennet's Foss near Malham, whilst across the county, they were especially thought to congregate around wells. For instance, the fairies were believed to wash their clothes in Claymore Well near Kettleness. On their washing days, their efforts to beat the linen dry with a battledore could supposedly be heard as far away as Runswick Bay.

A particularly famous watery encounter with the fairies occurred around 1815 at White Wells, an eighteenth-century spa-house on the edge of Ilkley Moor. The keeper at White Wells at that time was named William Butterfield, described by

Jennet's Foss near Malham, home of the Fairy Queen. (Kathryn Wilson)

somebody who had known him as 'a good sort of a man, honest, truthful and as steady and as respectable a fellow as you could find.' It was Butterfield's habit to open the door to the bathhouse at White Wells early in the day, but one midsummer morning when the birds were particularly active, he found the job unusually tricky. On that particular day, his key merely spun round in the lock and would not cause the lever to turn. At length, he admitted defeat and decided to apply brute force to the situation, but whilst he succeeded in pushing the door ajar, it was pushed right back again.

Losing his patience, Butterfield gave the door an almighty shove and it flung open to reveal a staggering sight:

> Whirr, whirr, whirr, such a noise and sight! All over the water and dipping into it was a lot of little creatures, dressed in green from head to foot, none of them more than eighteen inches high and making a chatter and a jabber thoroughly unintelligible. They seemed to be taking a bath, only they bathed with all their clothes on. Soon, however, one or two of them began to make off, bounding over the walls like squirrels.

Hoping to communicate with these strange creatures before they left, Butterfield greeted them, but inevitably this only provoked greater haste. 'Then away the whole tribe went, helter-skelter, toppling and tumbling, heads over heels, heels over heads, and all the while making a noise not unlike that of a disturbed nest of partridges.'

White Wells on Ilkley Moor, a fairies' bathing house? (Kai Roberts)

Of course, Ilkley Moor had long been known as a haunt of fairies. A cavity in the outcrop known as Hanging Stones, a small distance east along the moor from White Wells, had been called the Fairies' Parlour or Fairies' Kirk for centuries prior to Butterfield's account and according to local folklore, its tenants should not be disturbed. It is perhaps relevant that Hanging Stones is also the location of some fine examples of that enigmatic form of prehistoric rock-art known as cup-and-ring carvings. Indeed, Ilkley Moor bristles with such artefacts and with prehistoric archaeology generally. Once again, it seems that pre-modern man may have overtly associated the fairies with the visible relics of his pagan ancestors.

The fairies' pagan connotations may be one reason why they were so opposed to churches being built in their vicinity. This common migratory legend crops up at several places in Yorkshire including Holme-on-the-Wolds and a number of villages around Huddersfield – specifically Kirkheaton, Kirkburton and Thornhill. The church-builders are invariably warned that their favoured location in which to raise a new place of worship would not be favourably regarded by the fairies, but they ignore the advice and construct the church there anyway. Then just as they are nearing completion, they awake one morning to find everything demolished and the stones moved to a different place. They attempt to rebuild it on their chosen site but once again, their work is torn down and the materials shifted. Eventually, the builders admit defeat and simply build the church elsewhere.

In functional terms, this narrative probably accounted for cases where shifting patterns of land-use over the centuries had left the modern village centre at some distance from the local church. It is a story also connected with the Devil in some places (North Otterington and Leake, for instance) but whilst the Devil's motive is easily recognised as animosity towards Christianity, the fairies' intentions are a little more vague. Are they proclaiming their hostility to the new religion, or are they simply keen to be left alone? Given that their reticence is an almost universal theme in fairy lore, it may be the latter. Any form of disturbance seems to be resented by them and a church would certainly represent a substantial imposition.

Such behaviour could also be a product of their fondness for pranks and mischief: for whilst the fairies begrudge any human interference in *their* affairs, they seem happy to meddle with impunity in ours. Most famously, they were believed to enjoy firing arrows at cattle and so causing disease in the herd. Indeed, the earliest recorded mention of the fairies in England is an Anglo-Saxon charm against 'elf-shot'. Over 1,000 years later, Richard Blakeborough attested that this superstition was alive and well in Yorkshire, whilst it was even mentioned in Emily Brontë's *Wuthering Heights*. Yet again there is a connection with ancient man, as farmers regarded the prehistoric flint arrowheads often revealed by ploughing as evidence that fairies had been targeting their cattle. Touching the afflicted beasts with one of these flints was also considered to effect a cure.

Another game the fairies liked to play was to fling their 'butter' at the doors, gates and window-frames of a building, to which it would adhere and rot the wood away. Apparently the houses around Egton Grange were especially known for being thus targeted. Of course, 'fairy butter' was actually a common gelatinous fungus of the *Tremellales* order. Fungus is also implicated in the creation of 'fairy rings', circles of darkened grass which previous generations held to have been created by the fairies dancing overnight. In fact, it was caused by fungal mycelium beneath the surface of the soil, whose parasitic action on the grass leaves it in poorer condition than the surrounding field. Fairy Cross Plain in Fryupdale was renowned for its fairy rings which local children would dance around, taking care to circle fewer than nine times, lest the fairies gain power over them.

The fairies' need for human children is well known and once again, despite their aversion to humans intruding in their affairs, the fairies were more than happy to take great liberties when it came to ours. As the folklorist Katharine Briggs notes, 'So far as respect for human goods is concerned, honesty means nothing to fairies. They consider that they have a right to whatever they need or fancy, including the human beings themselves.' Indeed, they seemed to desperately require human children every now and then to keep the fairy stock healthy, and showed no qualms about stealing them as they chose, often leaving an unhealthy specimen of their own in the infant's place. This so-called 'changeling' is one of the most ubiquitous fairy motifs and undoubtedly arose to explain developmental disabilities in less enlightened ages.

The changeling belief appears to have been strong in Wharfedale during the early nineteenth century and the fairies of Almscliffe Crag were especially feared as

Almscliffe Crag in Wharfedale, home of child-stealing fairies. (Kathryn Wilson)

child-stealers. During the early part of that century, a farmer named Bradley lived in that region and he was convinced that three of his children were changelings. According to one source, 'Three of his sons, and two of the daughters were fine, tall men and women, who married early and well; but the three changelings were dwarfish, crooked and ill-tempered, and never married.' These three 'changelings' were still alive around the 1850s, and a writer for the *Leeds Mercury* in 1885 recalled gawping at Tom and Fanny Bradley during his childhood. Even then the rumour endured that their mother had left her real children unattended in the vicinity of Almscliffe Crag and had been left with changelings in their stead.

Fairies undoubtedly bore their own children. According to one report, a farm-girl once stumbled across such an infant on Fairy Cross Plain: 'It was lying in a swathe of half-made hay, as bonny a little thing as you'd ever seen. But it did not stay long with the lass that found it. It sort of dwindled away and she supposed the fairy-mother could do without it any longer.' Perhaps, however, they were not all as healthy as that one; or perhaps complications often developed during the birth, as one of the most curious requests fairies made of humans was for the services of a midwife. Again, this is an old and widespread migratory narrative, a version of which was recorded by Gervase of Tilbury in the twelfth century.

In Yorkshire, the legend is attached to Keighley market. One day, a stunted grey man approached a butter-wife at her stall in the town and pulled at her apron, gesturing that he needed her to assist his pregnant wife. The woman followed him, but curiously all those who saw her leave insisted that she had been alone and she retained no memory of the journey. At length, she found herself in a limestone cavern where she helped deliver a child from a similarly stunted and grey woman. Following the birth, the mother took a crystal phial and anointed the eyes of the infant; before she left, the butter-wife was sure to appropriate a drop for herself, knowing it to offer the gift of second sight.

The little man presently returned her to Keighley and left her with a bag of fairy gold for her trouble. But thanks to the liquid she had stolen, she had a greater reward: the ability to see the little people permanently. Unfortunately, it was not to last. Several weeks later, the butter-wife saw the stunted grey man again, stealing a bag of corn from the market. She asked after his wife and child, which startled the fairy and he jumped up on her stall. 'Which eye see you with?' he demanded, and the butter-wife pointed at the eye into which she'd dropped the liquid. The fairy then blew in that eye and vanished, after which the butter-wife never saw such a being again.

This story nicely exhibits the fairies' double standards; they were quite happy to exploit a human's midwifery skill and steal corn that men had harvested, but as soon as their own domain is threatened, they take action to eliminate the danger. Curiously, the fairy-midwife legend was clearly still circulating in the rural areas of North Yorkshire into the twentieth century. In a study of latter day fairy accounts, Katharine Briggs records the story of a district nurse who was supposedly taken by a diminutive man to deliver a child in a hut somewhere on Greenhow Hill – the wild expanse of moorland which rises between Wharfedale and Nidderdale. Naturally, she was never able to find this hut again.

That such a narrative survived into the last century is further proof of the enduring power of the fairy faith. As Katharine Briggs observes, 'English fairy beliefs … from Chaucer's time onwards have been supposed to belong to the last generation and to be lost to the present one. The strange thing is that rare, tenuous and fragile as it is, the tradition is still there and lingers on from generation to generation substantially unchanged.' Yet in some ways, it seems appropriate for the educated observer to regard fairy *belief* as a relic of the past, as it echoes the strong association between the fairies and the remains of our ancestors that prevailed amongst fairy believers themselves. Whatever the fairies might be, they have always existed on the fringes of the temporal landscape and perhaps they will continue to dwell on that threshold for many generations to come.

SIX

THE DEVIL

The Devil occupies a prominent place as an antagonist in the annals of local legend; a scarcely surprising position considering the emphasis which both medieval and post-Reformation Christianity gave to his persisting influence. Indeed, whilst most of the denizens with which folklore populated the countryside seem to have represented a parallel current of belief to Christianity and were often condemned by the Church, legends concerning the Devil may well have been sanctioned or even generated by ecclesiastic agencies. Whilst the subversive hand of vernacular belief can be detected in some of these narratives, by and large they appear consistent with the tenets of orthodox theology in England from the Middle Ages onwards.

In Yorkshire, the category in which the Devil most commonly appears is the landscape legend. Prominent topographic features and ancient megalithic structures are frequently attributed to the actions of His Satanic Majesty, much as they are sometimes attributed to the work of giants. For instance, like Wade, folklore credited the Devil with a supposedly Roman highway – in this case, Dhoul's Pavement which climbs over Blackstone Edge. The similarities between the Devil and giants in folklore are such that many have suggested that the Old Nick was imposed onto earlier indigenous giant legends, thereby creating a narrative more palatable to the Christian authorities. Discussing perceptions of prehistoric monuments in the medieval period, archaeologist Richard Hayman asserts, 'The Devil replaces giants in English folklore just as Arthur does in Welsh folklore.'

There are certainly some landscape features which are associated with both giants and the Devil, suggesting that the two narratives existed side-by-side and possibly their respective popularity was determined by class or locality. Almscliffe Crag in Wharfedale was supposed to have been thrown down either by the Devil

Dhoul's Pavement over Blackstone Edge, an ancient highway constructed by the Devil.
(Kai Roberts)

or by the giant Rombald's wife. Meanwhile, a stone at Scar Top in Netherton near Huddersfield, is imagined to bear the footprint of a Magdale giant, left as he frantically searched for his missing daughter (*See* Chapter Four); or alternatively the hoofmark of the Devil as he leapt from there to the summit of Castle Hill.

The Devil and giants also feature as rivals in some narratives. In one version of the legend, the rock which became Almscliffe Crag was originally thrown by the Devil at the giant Rombald during a fight on Ilkley Moor, overshooting its target by the substantial distance of eight miles. A little further north, the two adversaries pelted each other with rocks across Raydale. A stone thrown by the giant came to rest on the shore of Semer Water and is known as the Carlow Stone, whilst the stone hurled by Satan in response landed high on the slopes of Addleborough. Today, this earthfast boulder is still called the Devil's Stone and his claw marks are supposedly visible on the rock.

Such petrosomatoglyphs (supposed images of body parts imprinted in stone) are a common feature of both giant and Devil lore. In addition to Scar Top, the Devil also left his hoofmark on rocks at Baildon and Rivock Edge in West Yorkshire, both known as the Cloven Stones. These sites are not associated with detailed legends, but one unique tale from West Yorkshire relates how the Devil made a wager with God that he could stride across the Calder Valley from Stoodley Pike to Blackshaw Head. If he won the bet, he could claim all of the souls living in the dale below.

Great Rock in Calderdale, split by the Devil's cloven hoof. (Kai Roberts)

Fortunately for the folk of Hebden Bridge and neighbouring towns, just as he was at full stretch, the Devil lost his footing and tumbled down the valley side. As he fell, his hoof nicked the face of a huge gritstone buttress known as Great Rock and that cleft can still be seen running up its surface today.

Prehistoric burial cairns are also sites often associated with both giants and the Devil. Little Skirtful of Stones on Ilkley Moor is attributed to the giant Rombald's wife and His Satanic Majesty. A similar, albeit less well-preserved, Bronze-Age cairn called Devil's Apronful can be found on the moors above Appletreewick in Wharfedale. Legend tells that the Devil was carrying stones in his apron to fill up Dibb Gill across the valley, when he caught his foot on Nursery Knott and spilled them near Simon's Seat, where they still lie today. It is also said that if any of the stones are moved from this cairn, they will return to their original place overnight – a common motif in folklore connected with prehistoric monuments.

Yet, whilst local legend tends to credit giants with any immense topographic or megalithic feature, the folklorist Jacqueline Simpson has observed that sites associated with the Devil conform to a more noticeable pattern. She writes, 'Many legends ascribing landscape features to the malevolent or stupid actions of the Devil relate to unproductive areas and objects … Popular legends ascribing these unwelcome features to an evil or stupid being were a way of relieving God from the responsibility of having created them.' In Yorkshire, this tendency is even visible on a smaller scale, as farmers often called a poor stretch of pasture the 'Devil's field' and deliberately left it uncultivated so that the fiend would not interfere with the rest of the crops.

Examples of a larger topographic magnitude are also numerous. For instance, in the Colne and Holme Valleys, the barren and windswept summit of West Nab was considered to be the place where Satan had first set foot on earth. Meanwhile, sailors and fishermen along the Yorkshire coast regarded the rocky promontory of Filey Brigg – a dangerous impediment to shipping for centuries – as the 'Devil's creation'. Similarly, the natural amphitheatre known as the Hole of Horcum which once presented a laborious obstacle for travellers across the North York Moors, is colloquially named the 'Devil's Punchbowl'. Legend tells that it was scooped out by the Devil who meant to throw the earth at Scarborough. However, he was so startled by the sunlight glinting off Lilla Cross that he dropped the debris, which formed Blakey Topping.

The Hole of Horcum story exhibits another common motif in Devil lore: namely his almost comical stupidity and clumsiness. Whilst local legends often portray Satan working tirelessly against pious Christian towns, his schemes are invariably thwarted by his own ineptitude. Another such story is told of the Devil's attempt to throw a vast boulder at the village of Hartforth, just north of Richmond. He plucked the rock from the vicinity of Gilling, lifted it high above his head and declared, 'Have at thee, Black Harforth, but have a care of bonny Gilling!' But, as is so often the case in these tales, he substantially overshot his mark and the stone

West Nab near Meltham, where the Devil first set foot on earth. (Kai Roberts)

The Devil's Arrows at Boroughbridge, thrown by Satan himself. (Kai Roberts)

came to rest far beyond Hartforth, on the north side of Gatherley Moor. Again, his claw marks are supposedly imprinted on its surface.

Yet another example of the motif is connected to the Devil's Arrows, a row of three vast menhirs which lie beside the A1 near Boroughbridge. Standing up to 22 feet tall, they were probably erected during the Bronze Age, but, incredulous that ancient man could have been responsible for such a feat of engineering, medieval folklore found a different aetiology for them: they were thrown by the Devil at the nearby village of Aldborough from Howe Hill some eight miles in distance. As he cast them into the air, he proclaimed, 'Borobrigg, keep out o' th' way, for Auldboro' town I will ding down!' Of course, they came harmlessly to rest in fields between the two settlements and the Devil's purpose was frustrated once again.

In such narratives, the incompetence of the Devil emphasises the Christian lesson that the Devil had already been defeated by the actions of Christ, and that whilst he could tinker around, God would prevent him ever wreaking any serious damage. Jacqueline Simpson suggests that these tales may even have been transmitted by medieval priests themselves, who preached them as exempla. She writes, 'It becomes clear that every story in which the Devil tries to crush a church (or town) with a huge rock … but is foiled in the attempt, could once have been meant seriously as proof that God providentially saves the community from attacks by evil beings; the rock in question would mark the site of a religious event and would have a lesson to teach.'

The monolith in Rudston churchyard, also thrown by the Devil. (Kai Roberts)

If this supposition is correct, it would explain the incongruous case of the Rudston Monolith. At 25 feet, it is the tallest prehistoric menhir in Britain and the second tallest in Europe, but perhaps more remarkably it stands unmolested in the churchyard at Rudston in East Yorkshire. Antiquaries have long wondered how such a significant pagan symbol was tolerated for so long in the immediate vicinity of a church. Many have suggested that the church was built beside it to maintain continuity with an older place of worship. Yet perhaps the true answer lies in a familiar legend told about the monolith; that the Devil threw it there in an attempt to destroy Rudston Church. If Simpson is correct, the monument would have provided clergy at the church with an excellent concrete illustration of the Devil's crude malignancy and the providence of God.

Some commentators have argued that the early medieval Church associated prehistoric monuments with the Devil in order to demonise the pagan practices which took place there, and so impel the heathens towards Christianity. It was a popular assertion amongst early folklorists and is often repeated by more recent writers of a neo-pagan bent, yet there is very little evidence to support such a hypothesis. Where studies were conducted into the association between the Devil and prehistoric stone circles in the south-west of England, the connection was found to be no older than the seventeenth century in most cases, long after Christianity had firmly established itself and the pagan rituals conducted at the circles had been forgotten.

Roulston Crag and Hood Hill, between which the Devil leapt. (Kai Roberts)

Only one legend in Yorkshire overtly associates the Devil with paganism and whilst it partly corresponds to a certain familiar type of narrative, there is reason to believe that it has been greatly romanticised by eighteenth- or nineteenth-century collectors. The tale recorded by Thomas Gill in 1852 relates that the area beneath Sutton Bank in the Hambleton Hill, known as Happy Valley, was once a refuge for 'Druids' who sought to continue practicing their religion unhindered by the spread of Christianity, but at length, their fastness was penetrated by a Christian missionary who challenged the Druids to a debate to settle the question of the superior religion.

This debate took place at the foot of a rocky escarpment known as Roulston Crag, where the Devil had disguised himself as one of the Druids who were to speak in favour of their faith. 'The Evil One placed his foot on one of those mountain rocks, and being foiled in his arguments by the powerful reasoning of the missionary, flapped his brazen wings and fled across the valley with the stone adhering to his feet, the heat of which melted a hole in the top until he came to the ridge of Hood Hill where he dropped the massive block.' The Hood Hill Stone still lies on the wooded slopes of this eminence, whilst the narrow pass between Roulston Crag and the summit of Hood Hill is known as Devil's Leap.

However, anybody trying to claim this legend as proof that early Christians explicitly associated pagan religions with the Devil is going to be hard pressed. Whilst the motif of the Devil leaping from Roulston Crag to Hood Hill and depositing a hoof-marked stone there is likely to have been an indigenous tradition, the remainder exhibits all the hallmarks of antiquarian invention. It is improbable that the term 'Druid' would have been widely known amongst the populace prior to the eighteenth century, when it was popularised by the likes of William Stukeley. Furthermore, there is no evidence to suggest that Druidism survived beyond the Roman occupation; when Christian missionaries such as Paulinus arrived in North Yorkshire, they encountered Saxon, rather than Celtic, paganism.

Indeed, it may be that many legends featuring the Devil did not emerge until considerably later than England's conversion to Christianity. Unlike many supernatural entities, Protestantism was comfortable with folk belief concerning the arch-fiend, and it may be that such legends were actually a product of the post-Reformation period. As the landscape historian Alexandra Walsham notes, 'Protestantism was not inherently opposed to the notion that ugly and unproductive features of the natural environment might be the work of God's eternal enemy … Such stories were hardly inconsistent with the renewed emphasis Lutheran and Calvinist thought placed on the terrifying power and might of Satan.'

Whilst the provenance of his role in landscape legends remains an open question, the more overtly moralistic legends involving the Devil have more than a hint of Puritanism about them. Across the county, a number of places associated with licentious behaviour seem to have been cast as a favourite haunt of Satan. For instance, in the seventeenth and eighteenth centuries, the secluded Cock Mill in Eskdale was a notorious haven for drinking, card games and cockfighting; prompting one writer to record that 'a certain gentleman in black often took his seat amongst the rest and appeared very much interested in the game and it is even said that when one person was looking under the table for a lost card he, to his great horror, spied two cloven feet.'

Similarly, the stone at Scar Top in Netherton which supposedly bore the Devil's hoof print, was once well known as a rogues' retreat. A local historian wrote, 'This spot was notorious in early nineteenth century days; on Sundays it was the scene of gambling schools playing pitch and toss; on winter weeknights it was the rendezvous of unruly youths ever ready to pass rude remarks to casual pedestrians.' It is not hard to imagine some brimstone preacher (the area was a hotbed of Methodism at the time) grafting the figure of Satan onto an earlier giant legend concerning Scar Top in order to demonise that place and those who congregated there.

However, we need not think it was only the clergy who propagated such tales. As Charlotte Burne wrote, 'The study of the Bible by the poor has had much to do with extinguishing certain phases of folklore and keeping alive others.' One example of this may be a tale concerning the Devil associated with the hamlet of Roydhouse, which lies on the moors to the south-east of Huddersfield. During the mid-eighteenth century, the settlement was home to a lawyer by the name of Wright, universally despised in the region for his miserly nature and ruthless transactions. He was the sort of man who happily extorted money from the 'fatherless, widows and the poor' whilst never giving back a single penny to the community. Thus, no tears were shed when one night the villain vanished and was never seen again.

It was not long before local gossip claimed that Wright's soul belonged to the Devil and the price had finally been exacted. It was rumoured that Satan had 'arrived in a coach, drawn by two horses breathing fire from their nostrils and leaping twelve yards at every step' – to drag the lawyer off 'moaning and groaning and bewailing his fate'. Nobody dared enter the room from which he had supposedly been taken until many decades had passed and apparently when the door was finally breached, the dust was discovered lying three inches thick across the room and a chest containing Wright's documents still stood in one corner.

It is perhaps incongruous that the fallen angel, Lucifer, should become the agent of God's judgement when in all other matters he opposes divine will, but this was a paradox of orthodox theology as much as folk belief, and fear that the Devil would claim the soul of wrongdoers extended well into the nineteenth century in Yorkshire. Indeed, it was responsible for a quite an extraordinary episode at Wilsden in West Yorkshire, sometime in the mid-1800s, when following a series of petty thefts in the village – including a pair of scissors from one house – the local worthies summoned a man named Professor Bombost from Huddersfield; who proclaimed he would invoke the Devil to root the miscreant out.

A crowd gathered to watch Bombost chalk a circle on the ground, in the centre of which he placed some smouldering substance and proceeded to recite an incantation. Suddenly, from the opposite end of the square, a luminous figure emerged with fire issuing from his hands and mouth. This fearsome vision declared, in a suspiciously local accent: 'If them as stolen t'scissors doesn't bring 'em back to t'woman 'at belongs 'em before a fortnight's gone by, when they comes to die I'll make their bones roll about in their graves for evermore, and their souls shall know no peace!' With a terrible shriek, the figure then disappeared into the darkness and the terrified villagers fled to their homes. A few days later, the scissors were returned to their owner in the night.

Of course, even as an agent of retribution, the Devil is frequently shown to be impotent and, as with many folk narratives, the fiend is outwitted by an ordinary man. A story from the North York Moors tells how the Devil tried to take refuge from a storm one night at the Saltersgate Inn, which stands beside a stretch of road known as the Devil's Elbow, not far from the Hole of Horcum. However, a priest was already a guest at the hostelry and tried to banish the interloper with a rite of exorcism. This had little effect but to drive the Devil into the kitchen, from where he could not be removed, and he threatened to inflict all manner of misfortune upon the inn and its tenants for their lack of courtesy.

But the landlord of the Saltersgate Inn succeeded where the priest had failed; he managed to impede the baleful influence by lighting a peat fire, which trapped the Prince of Darkness in its smoke and prevented him carrying out any mischief. It was said that if the peat fire should ever be extinguished, the Devil would be free to bring ruin on the building and by the end of the twentieth century, that fire was believed to have burned continuously for at least 200 years. Unfortunately, like so many pubs in the last decade, the Saltersgate Inn recently went out of business and its ever-burning flame was finally quenched. At the time of writing, the Devil's judgement has come to pass and the once-thriving coaching inn is reduced to a derelict shell.

The most common stories of native wit triumphing over the Devil's wiles can be found attached to a number of bridges across the country. Indeed, tales of bridges constructed by the Devil are a classic example of a migratory legend, and so many such sites exist that it is now impossible to say which location provided the original model for this narrative, although the most famous examples are found just over the Cumbrian border at Kirkby Lonsdale and in Ceredigion in Wales. In Yorkshire, a story corresponding almost exactly to these legends is found associated with Kilgram Bridge, which crosses the River Ure near Masham, and was probably constructed by the Cistercian monks of Jervaulx Abbey during the twelfth century.

The bridge replaced an earlier ford over the river but one that was particularly vulnerable to flooding, much to the inconvenience of the local inhabitants. One day, as they were bemoaning this state of affairs, the Devil sauntered along and promised to construct a bridge for them, on the condition that he could claim the soul of the first living thing to cross it. The country folk accepted his bargain but spent many long hours debating who should be their sacrifice to Satan, until a cunning old shepherd spoke up with a solution. The shepherd owned a dog called Grim and once the Devil had completed his work, the old man swam to the far side of the river and whistled for his dog to follow. Grim obediently trotted across the bridge and the poor hound was claimed by the Devil for his prize. The bridge has been known as 'Kill Grim Bridge' ever since.

That the Devil should be associated with so many bridges in Britain suggests this narrative must have encoded a once-relevant message, yet it is now unclear why His Satanic Majesty should so often be credited with building these structures. Indeed, such legends seem to represent a counter-example to Jacqueline Simpson's contention that features associated with the Devil tend to be unproductive; for whilst the terrain crossed by these bridges often fits that description, the bridges themselves are anything but. The theme of duping the Devil is doubtless important – as getting one over on a seemingly invincible adversary is a common trope in folklore and seems to have acted as an expression of local community pride – but why one of the favourite vehicles for such narratives should be the 'Devil's bridge' legend remains an open question.

Moreover, in the legend's basic form, there is not even any element of trickery: the Devil is simply credited with building the bridge during the night, before he is interrupted by the dawn and leaves the edifices in a shabby state. This tale is told of two sites in North Yorkshire: Butterton Bridge near Sawley, built in the thirteenth century by the monks of Fountains Abbey; and the original Hell Gill Bridge, which crosses a tributary of the River Ure as it plunges through a treacherous ravine on the flanks of High Abbotside. The antiquity of these structures suggests the legend may simply have arisen as a result of later generations' incredulity that their ancestors could have been responsible for such feats of engineering. This echoes the attribution of prehistoric megaliths to giants, but perhaps they believed bridges required the Devil's more powerful intellect.

Perhaps the most unique example of such a legend in Yorkshire concerns Dibble's Bridge above Appletreewick in Wharfedale, in which the 'Father of Lies' behaves entirely honourably. The story relates that a cobbler from Thorpe, by the name of Ralph Calvert, was returning from Fountains Abbey, where he had been to sell his wares. His route home took him across Appletreewick Moor and forced him to cross a dismal ravine cut by the River Dibb, as it flowed down to join the Wharfe in the valley below. Ralph found the atmosphere of this gorge so ominous that he was forced to strike up a song to fortify himself as he went. The tune he selected was a popular one at the time describing the meeting between a miller and the Devil. But his courage soon dwindled when he heard another voice join him on the final couplet.

Ralph was soon heartened again when he saw that his fellow traveller was a distinguished looking gentlemen, and they soon struck up a lively conversation in that gloomy place. At length, the cobbler even offered to share some of his lunch and whisky with his new companion. Once they had both finished their repast, the stranger said that he must introduce himself and all of Ralph's terror returned when the name he gave was 'Satan'. However, the Devil told him that he had nothing to fear; indeed he was now in the cobbler's debt for the hospitality he had been shown and wondered how he might repay the favour. Ralph answered that he would quite like a bridge built across the ravine which they had both just crossed. The Devil agreed and told him that the task would be completed in four days time.

Upon arriving home, Ralph told his wife all about the encounter and soon the tale was all around the village, prompting a great deal of ridicule. Thus, when the fourth day arrived, a sizeable party of local folk accompanied Ralph back to the ravine to see if the Devil had been true to his word. And sure enough, they discovered a new bridge, one which all those assembled agreed was as fine a specimen as they had ever seen. The village priest even agreed that it could be crossed without fear of diabolic molestation, although he sprinkled a little holy water and erected a cross at each end, just to be on the safe side. A Puritan minister pulled down the crosses during the Commonwealth, but the name remains as a testament to the structure's creation. Originally it was called Devil's Bridge, but over the years that title has been corrupted and now it is known just as Dibble's Bridge.

It may be that the Devil has become attached to these bridges through folk etymology alone. Needless to say, Dibble is not a corruption of Devil at all, but comes from the Old English 'dybbel', meaning 'bridge over the pool'. Similarly, Kilgram

Dibble Bridge in Wharfedale, constructed by the Devil. (Kai Roberts)

Bridge is actually derived from the Old Norse 'Kelgrim haugr' meaning 'Kelgrim's mound'. Even Hell Gill, which seems a natural association for such a Stygian abyss, is more likely to be an Old Norse appellation meaning 'flat-stoned ravine'. As such, these stories (with the exception of Butterton) are all back-formations to account for curious names; the true meaning of which have long since been forgotten.

However, this still does not explain why they were associated with the Devil specifically; after all, 'Kilgram' or even 'Kill Grim' does not necessarily lend itself to such a connection. In this regard, a common feature which might be relevant is their association with monasteries. Kilgram and Butterton Bridges were constructed under the aegis of Jervaulx and Fountains Abbey respectively, and may have been associated with monastic traffic for many centuries thereafter. Similarly, Fountains Abbey is mentioned in the legend of Dibble's Bridge and crosses were supposed to have stood at each end, until they were pulled down by a Puritan cleric in the seventeenth century. Could the connection with the Devil have arisen from a post-Reformation inclination to demonise the relics of their Popish forebears?

Yet, it seems the impulse may go deeper than this. Increasingly, folklorists have recognised that 'liminal' spaces were regarded as especially spiritually dangerous by the pre-modern mind. Such places were seen as thresholds which Otherworldy visitors could cross as easily as ourselves, and water-crossings were an archetypally liminal location. Indeed, bridges were doubly perilous as not only were they thresholds, they crossed water, itself a supernatural medium. Folklore records bridges as a particularly common location for uncanny encounters: ghosts, boggarts and barguests all frequented water-crossings, and apotropaic measures were often taken by locals to counteract their influence – from foundation sacrifices to carved heads (*See* Chapter Two).

Hence, it is perhaps not surprising that the Devil is so frequently connected with bridges. Such crossing-places are associated with malign influences in countless cultures and evidently folk-Christianity was no different in this respect. However useful the bridge may be, it was a significantly liminal space where the soul was always at risk. Suggesting that these structures were built by Satan ably expresses such anxiety; perhaps more instructively, those stories in which the Devil is tricked out of his due or builds the bridge honourably, represent a way of assuaging those anxieties. They communicate that whilst the fiend once tried to claim a named bridge for his dominion, he had been thwarted and it was now safe for good Christian souls to cross for evermore.

SEVEN
PHANTOM HOUNDS

One of the most familiar tropes of British folklore, examples of the 'phantom hound' that portends misfortune, can be found in numerous counties across the United Kingdom. The phenomenon is perhaps most familiar by its East Anglian name 'Black Shuck' and as the motif which inspired Sir Arthur Conan Doyle's classic novel, *The Hound of the Baskervilles*, or the 'Grim' in J.K. Rowling's popular Harry Potter series. In Yorkshire, however, it is primarily known by the names barguest (sometimes spelled barghest), padfoot, guytrash and skriker. There does not seem to be any geographical pattern determining use of the names, and indeed, they are sometimes used interchangeably to refer to the same example.

This chapter will employ the generic term 'phantom hound' or whichever name was used in the original record on the grounds that they all broadly belong to the same category, although even this statement is controversial. Nearly everything about the phantom hound is ambiguous and liminal, forever slipping through attempts to define or classify it. It is perhaps best to consider the motif in terms of Ludwig Wittgenstein's 'family resemblance' theory, whereby each instantiation of a phenomenon draws its characteristics from a common pool, but whilst many examples will overlap in the features they exhibit, very few will be identical.

It is even unclear exactly what *sort* of entity the phantom hound is supposed to represent. Is it a ghostly apparition, a demonic fiend or an anomalous, but nonetheless, physical beast? At times it seems to be able to interact with the corporeal world, at other times it cannot. In some places, the thing seems to have a definite purpose, whilst elsewhere it merely lurks in the shadows of the local psyche, a nebulous bogeyman which crudely embodies all the terrors of the night.

The only thing that seems certain is that its presence was universally regarded as ominous; a source of nocturnal terror across Yorkshire in earlier centuries.

The archetype of the phenomenon is an unnaturally large black dog, with long, shaggy hair and glowing eyes 'as large as tea plates'. For instance, in his influential 1879 work, *Notes on the Folk-lore of the Northern Counties of England and the Borders*, William Henderson describes the padfoot around Leeds as 'the size of a small donkey, black with shaggy hair and large eyes like saucers' and many other accounts feature a similar depiction. The fiend was also supposed to 'utter a roar totally unlike the voice of any known animal' and walk with a distinctive 'shog … shog … shog' sound. In some places it appeared with a long, rattling chain attached to its legs. Doubtless, it was these aural attributes that earned it names such a skriker and padfoot.

However, even this model varies considerably. The taxonomy of 'phantom black dogs' is very much the product of Victorian folklorists, who, in thrall to the natural sciences' mania for classification in the nineteenth century, were ever eager to shoehorn a diverse array of phenomena into a single unwieldy category. As a result, it is unclear if the name given to individual examples – whether it be barguest, guytrash, padfoot or skriker – was the common local term, or simply the preferred category of the folklorist who collected the story.

Similarly, it is hard to tell whether the phantom hound was the most common manifestation of this being, or merely the classification it most closely fitted in the mind of the collector. For in several stories, the same names are used to refer to things which take other forms, animal or otherwise. In an unpublished work, Branwell Brontë refers to the guytrash as 'a spectre not at all similar to the ghosts of those who were once alive, nor to fairies, nor to demons … (mostly) a black dog dragging a chain, a dusky calf, nay, even a rolling stone.' Meanwhile, as the folklorist Jeremy Harte observes, 'Behind the standard phrases which describe these apparitions – "as large as a donkey", "as big as a calf", "shaggy as a bear" – there are traces of earlier stories in which they had actually been bears, calves and donkeys.'

In some instances, the phenomenon was actually multiform. For example, one story from Almondbury tells of a man who encountered the padfoot 'like a hound dog, all white; he tried to coax it but it turned into a calf … When he got below it turned into a bear and began to roll all the way down.' Even more bizarrely, the Holden Rag, which haunted the moorlands of upper Calderdale around the West Yorkshire/Lancashire border, 'was said to appear sometimes in the form of a great black dog and at other times as a rag of white linen on a thorn … which always eluded the grasp of mortal hands, shrivelling up and vanishing in a flash.'

It seems that Branwell Brontë's interpretation was influenced by a tradition attached to Ponden Hall at Stanbury, a few miles from his family home in Haworth. This spirit variously took the form of a 'shadowy greybeard carrying a lantern' or 'a flaming barrel which rolled down the fields and past the house' and was regarded as an omen of ill-potent.

In this respect, the phantom hound and its relatives seem to be a corrupted descendant of the shape-changing apparitions which were a common motif of medieval superstition. In the early fifteenth century, an anonymous monk at Byland Abbey in North Yorkshire recorded some notable examples of such revenants from around the region. One manifestation went through a series of transformations from a crow into a 'dog with a chain on its neck'; next into 'a shape of flame, transparent, and words came not from its lips but from its centre'; then into a 'goat which went round ... moaning'; and finally became 'the shape of a man of great stature, lean and spine-chilling to look at.'

Taking these various concerns into account, it is perhaps more fruitful to look for commonalities in the function of these apparitions, rather than their formal characteristics. As previously mentioned, the only universal attribute of phantom hounds is that they were once widely feared and it was generally held that to encounter one was a very risky business, although once again the reasons for this dread can differ. Sometimes the terror seems to have derived from the physical harm the entity could inflict, whilst on other occasions it was because such an encounter was an augury of disaster for the witness, his loved ones or his neighbourhood.

Perhaps the best-known example of the phantom hound in Yorkshire was certainly capable of causing bodily injury. This fearsome barguest was supposed to dwell in a deep and treacherous limestone ravine known as Trollers Gill, in Wharfedale. A local ballad, first recorded by William Hone in 1827, relates that after a good many drinks, the sceptical John Lambert of Skyreholme vowed to confront the fiend. He made his way to the gorge at midnight and called on the demon dog. At this, a storm brewed up, then suddenly:

> A dreadful thing from the cliff did spring
> And its wild bark thrilled around –
> Its eyes had the glow of the fires below
> 'Twas the form of the spectral hound.

The following morning Lambert's corpse was discovered at the bottom of the gill:

> And marks were impressed on the dead man's breast
> But they seemed not by mortal hand.

Belief in the barguest of Trollers Gill was still clearly common in Wharfedale a century after this ballad was chronicled by Hone. Writing in 1929, Halliwell Sutcliffe – a resident of nearby Linton – relates the experience of a cobbler from Fountains who met the barguest, when he stumbled into Trollers Gill after losing his way over Greenhow Hill one night. The wayfarer told how, 'the dog came out into the moonlight, big as a littlish bear ... with great eyes like saucers. He'd a shaggy sort of

Trollers Gill in Wharfedale, haunt of a fearsome barguest. (Kai Roberts)

smell as he went by, and I counted myself for dead. But he chanced not to glimpse me, praise all the saints that ever were.'

Less terminal traditions are also recorded. Henderson writes of the widespread belief that 'if anyone came in its way, the barguest would strike out and inflict a wound that would never heal'. Meanwhile, a close encounter with the Almondbury padfoot was thought to cause paralysis of the arms. If one wished to escape unharmed, it seems to have been prudent to ignore the padfoot as far as possible, for one source claimed, 'A word or blow gave the creature power over you; a story is told of a man who … kicked the thing and was forthwith dragged along through the hedge and ditch to his home and left under the window.'

Evading a barguest or padfoot was invariably a difficult feat and Halliwell Sutcliffe's cobbler is a rare example of someone who succeeded. They moved with uncanny speed and agility, 'padding lightly at the rear of a person and within a stretch of thought would be in front of them or at their side.' Keeping an eye on the brute was similarly challenging. The prolific West Riding historian, J. Horsfall Turner, recorded that the guytrash, 'when followed by an individual … begins to walk backwards with his eyes fixed full on his pursuer and vanished at the slightest momentary inattention.'

Moreover, attempting to escape a phantom hound that had already marked you for its attention seems to have been a futile endeavour, as fate would always intervene. Reverend J.C. Atkinson relates the story of a young man who was walking home

The old cemetery at Egton, where a donkey-shaped barguest once lurked. (Kai Roberts)

drunk one night and chanced upon the donkey-shaped barguest that haunted the vicinity of St Hilda's Church in Egton. Seeking to cross the cemetery on his route, he found the way blocked by the fiend, who thwarted his every attempt to pass through the gate. The youth proceeded to evade the thing by following a nearby lane and climbing into the churchyard from there. Yet all his cunning proved in vain, for as he crossed the hallowed ground in darkness, he stumbled into an open grave and broke his neck.

It seems that if the barguest did not do harm itself, then it often presaged death or 'betokened evil'. The tragedy it foretold did not necessarily have to befall the witness or his family, but often appeared to folk upon the death of some local worthy. This was certainly the case with the guytrash at Horton near Bradford. Victorian antiquary, William Cudworth, relates the story of a man who encountered the fiend 'jumping at his heels' as he walked past the gates of the now-demolished Horton Hall in the 'witching hour'. At the sight of the hound, the man fled home as fast he could and collapsed into a faint. The following day, he learnt that the master of Horton Hall had died around the same time as he had seen the guytrash.

In some stories, the appearance of such a fiend coincides with the death of a particularly hated figure in the community. Whilst this might seem like a positive omen for the local populace, the resultant manifestation often went on to terrorise the neighbourhood every bit as much as their lately deceased persecutor – such as in the story of the guytrash which appeared in the guise of a black goat following the demise of the reviled Julian of Goathland. In another instance, a barguest in the shape of a black pig was witnessed in York following the execution of the notorious witch and poisoner, Mary Bateman, in 1809.

The association with death can also be found in the tendency of phantom hounds to haunt the vicinity of graveyards or the route of old corpse ways. Some Victorian etymologists even suggested that the word 'barguest' might derive from the German *bahre geist*, meaning 'spirit of the bier' (a bier being the stand on which a corpse or coffin was situated). The nineteenth-century fondness for comparative mythology also connected phantom hounds with the Scandinavian 'church-grim', a guardian spirit thought to have been derived from a dog buried alive as a foundation sacrifice when the church was built.

There are also pronounced similarities to a superstition known as the Gabble Ratchets (sometimes referred to as the Gabriel Hounds), thought to be an airborne pack of hideous and sometimes human-headed spectral dogs, whose 'gabbling' cry was once a source of great terror throughout the northern counties of England. The sound was variously described as 'a great number of whelps barking and howling' and like 'the questing of a dozen beagles on the foot of a race.' To hear their cacophony passing over your house was widely regarded as a sure harbinger of disaster.

Belief in the Gabble Ratchets seems to have persisted for many centuries, even in the more industrialised areas of the county. The nonconformist firebrand and prolific diarist, Reverend Oliver Heywood, recorded the tradition around Halifax in 1664, and more than two centuries later, in 1879, William Henderson found it was still current amongst the denizens of Sheffield and Leeds. He also noted that around the latter city, the Gabble Ratchets were thought to be the unhappy souls of babies who had died before they could be baptised and as a consequence were unable to enter the portals of Heaven.

A number of other animal apparitions acted as premonitions of death around Yorkshire, and whilst they may not have been recorded under the name barguest, padfoot or guytrash, they performed an identical role and were held in similar awe. For instance, in South Yorkshire, 'It is always an unlucky omen and frequently a sign of death to see the Grey Cat. This spectre is tall and very thin, with big, round, flashing eyes and it always appears in the dusk of an evening.' Then there's Elland in West Yorkshire, haunted by 'a ghostly white mouse which visited Long Wall after dark; it was said that whoever saw it was sure to meet with some misfortune.' Or Cowling in Craven, home to 'a white rabbit that is seen to cross the road at Ickornshaw in a most eerie way and considered an omen of evil portent.'

Inevitably, unscrupulous characters took advantage of the dread surrounding such harbingers and faked manifestations were not unknown. Felgreave Wood near Huddersfield was once known as the haunt of 'a dog possessing a human head and a beard stretching from ear to ear' and in the mid-nineteenth century a woman named Elizabeth Haigh supposedly fainted after witnessing this 'monstrosity', to be found the following day in a dire condition. However, it transpired that the local gamekeepers were merely exploiting an existing legend and dressing in sheepskins to crawl around the woods at night as a deterrent against superstitious poachers!

Meanwhile, the wags of Threshfield in Wharfedale thought it a great lark to dress a particularly large goat in a rattling chain, and let it loose to roam the lanes at night, much to the terror of farmers returning from the market at Kettlewell. It is said that one notoriously dishonest individual encountered the creature and fearing it was a barguest, got down on his knees and begged God to deliver him, promising to mend his ways in the future. He eventually managed to evade the disguised goat and was from that time considerably more honourable in his dealings – at least until he discovered the truth of the ruse.

Phantom hounds, and associated apparitions, seem to have been held in such fear that 'nothing more effectively cleared the streets by night than the report that t'guytrash was out.' Even in relatively populous centres such as Leeds or Skipton, a rumour that the padfoot was abroad would deter people from venturing any distance alone in the dark. In more lonely, rural areas there were often spots – such as the Rudgate at Walton or a bridge near Parlington – that were considered no-go areas after sunset.

Antiquarians initially seem to have perceived the phantom hound as an urban phenomenon. The earliest recorded instances in Yorkshire are the barguest of York and the padfoot of Pontefract, whilst an especially intimidating example was chronicled around Wakefield in 1766 – described as 'shagged like a bear, as big as a calf, strange horns of unusual form, clanking a chain from one of its hind legs.' It seems that during the eighteenth century, nearly every city street had its own guardian barguest, padfoot, guytrash or skriker, each as distinctive as the thoroughfare itself.

However, as the nineteenth century wore on, folklorists grew less and less interested in the industrialised urban areas and focused their attention primarily on rural populations, believing that ancient lore survived most authentically in places unsullied by technological advancement. As a result, towards the end of that century, the printed evidence suggests that phantom hounds had forsaken their municipal haunts for the tranquillity of the countryside. It is difficult to tell if this purely reflects the bias of the collectors or changing beliefs amongst the urban masses. Certainly some correspondents seem to suggest the latter. The guytrash was said to have left Horton when the district was incorporated, as it had grown 'jealous of the policemen'!

In towns, the phantom hound seems to have been regarded as the *genius loci* of individual streets. It especially appears to have been associated with districts of ill-repute. For instance, the barguest of York favoured the vicinity of the prison and the gallows, whilst in Almondbury, the padfoot was believed to haunt the area around the 'gang doors', notorious in the town as a gathering place for ruffians and ne'er-do-wells. As such, the malevolent hound embodies the character of the locale and the belief performs a social function by deterring respectable citizens from straying too close to these dens of iniquity.

Similarly, in rural areas the phantom hound is often found in connection with dangerous places. The barguest of Trollers Gill in Wharfedale is a fine illustration of this relationship and writer, Edmund Bogg, spells it out in the story of an acquaintance travelling to Skyreholme at night during a storm:

> Amid the roar of the elements he was completely lost. In fear and trembling, hurrying onwards, not knowing whither, two more steps and he would have dropped 100 feet into a boiling torrent below. But, at that moment … a brilliant flash of lightning illuminated the scene – sufficient to disclose the hideous chasm. Shuddering with horror, he managed to drag himself from the brink; then falling to the ground, he lay until the storm had spent its fury. In the grey dawn … he managed to drag himself home, profoundly glad to have escaped the jaws of the Spectral Hound.

In Bogg's narrative, the precipitous limestone gorge is the barguest and vice-versa, and a slavering, demonic hound certainly makes an appropriate personification of this forbidding landscape. Equally, phantom hounds are frequently recorded in close proximity to hazardous bodies of water – old ponds, wells, river-crossings and the like. J. Horsfall Turner notes that in the West Riding, the guytrash was often seen to retreat into rivers or pools of water, and believed the name 'guytrash' came from the splashing sound of its feet.

At Kirk Deighton in North Yorkshire, a black dog was thought to walk around the village pond at the time of the full moon, whilst at Thornton near Bradford, a guytrash known as the Bloody Tongue would emerge from Jim Craven's Well and stalk down to the stream to drink. It was memorably described as 'a great dog with startling red eyes, a tail as big as the branch of a tree and a lolling tongue that dripped blood. When he drank from the beck the water ran red right past the bridge.'

Moreover, such watery locations were not just physically perilous, but spiritually so as well. In pre-modern thought, water – especially water-crossings and springs that emerge mysteriously from the earth – was regarded as fundamentally liminal. To a holistic worldview, which comprehends much in terms of correspondences and sympathies, such material thresholds were also perceived as less-corporeal boundaries, where this world presses close against the Other. Consequently they were considered prime spots for unearthly encounters, and precisely the sort of place an entity like the phantom hound was most likely to lurk.

Ivelet Bridge in Swaledale, guarded by a phantom hound. (Kai Roberts)

The barguest that was sometimes seen on Ivelet Bridge across the River Swale in North Yorkshire, seemed to embody all the most common associations of the phantom hound motif. Not only did it haunt an ancient water-crossing, but the bridge was once a stopping point on a corpse way from Upper Swaledale to the parish church at Grinton. There is even a stone built into the bridge on which coffins were rested. The phantom hound was said 'to glide silently on to the bridge and disappear over the ledge' and unsurprisingly, a sighting of this particular example was widely regarded as 'a sign of some tragic event to come'.

For the most part, however, a first-hand sighting of the phantom hound seems to have been a rare thing. The Victorian antiquarians, topographers and folklorists who recorded these beliefs were mostly of the opinion that they were already dying out, and any actual eyewitness accounts (or 'memorates') tended to be the experiences of deceased relatives, friends-of-friends, or had occurred many decades earlier and were recalled dimly through the haze of memory. Mostly phantom hounds were recorded only as 'rumour legends', firmly attached to some specific locale and superstition, but devoid of any more extensive narrative.

There are rare exceptions, of course. The legend of Trollers Gill is an obvious example, but this largely conforms to a migratory legend-type found throughout Britain, in which a sceptical (and often inebriated) individual sets out to confront a supernatural phenomenon which is widely feared in the neighbourhood and swiftly comes to regret it. Some more unique examples exist, but it is often difficult to tell to what extent they were genuine local legends and to what extent they were embellished or romanticised by their collectors, using elements of conventional ghost lore. The following example invokes so many folkloric tropes that it seems a little too self-consciously crafted to be 'authentic'. However, it is also one of the most remarkable and macabre legends in the canon of Yorkshire folklore, and is worth relating in full for that reason.

The narrative takes place around Goathland on the North York Moors ostensibly in the early medieval period, as the local lord, Julian de Mauley, is described as somebody who still subscribed to the pagan religion of the Vikings. Julian was a particularly ruthless and despised ruler who, prior to the construction of his new castle at Julian Park, decided to secure its future stability through the ancient custom of foundation sacrifice. To this end, he seized a beautiful maiden called Gytha and instructed that she be walled up alive in the base of the castle, forcing her father Gundrun to do the job. In a final act of cruelty, Julian provided Gytha with a spinning-wheel to while away the time until her inevitable death, jibing that a woman must be kept busy until her very end.

The following year, on the eve of the anniversary of the sacrifice, unearthly cries began to reverberate through the castle walls from their foundations. As Julian lay in his chamber, they grew louder and louder, seeming to draw ever closer, until at last a white wraith clutching a spindle manifested at the foot of his bed. Insensible with terror, the tyrant could only lay there whilst the apparition began to bind his legs with thread from her spindle. Although the fibres were invisible, he was unable to break them and the next morning, long after the spirit had departed, he found he remained permanently lame.

Each year on that grim anniversary, the spectre would visit Julian; binding a little more of his body with that supernatural thread and each year, the paralysis and pain grew worse. Neither medical intervention, nor confession of sin, brought him respite – even his conversion to Christianity and construction of a new church in Goathland was in vain. Eventually, after a decade or so, his entire body had succumbed to the affliction and he finally expired, wracked with pain and no longer able to draw breath.

At first, the people of Goathland thought their troubles had finally come to an end: the brutal Julian de Mauley was dead and they were finally free from his reign of terror. However, shortly after his demise, a new terror began to stalk the countryside thereabouts, especially the vicinity of the new church. The fiend was described as 'a gigantic black goat, with eyes that burned like live coals and horns tipped with fire', and whosoever encountered this guytrash was seized by a mysterious malady and died in a matter of days. Its origin was unclear, but many believed it was the spirit of Julian de Mauley perpetuating his evil from beyond the grave.

Meanwhile, the dreadful cries of the spinning ghost still echoed from Julian's abandoned castle and always seemed to foretell the death of a local girl. The beleaguered locals initially turned to the Church for help but to no avail, and their predicament grew so grave that they were forced to consult a local witch, known as the Spaewife of Fylingdales. She did not give her advice easily but hinted that the

Julian Park near Goathland, haunt of the terrifying guytrash. (Kai Roberts)

only way to be permanently rid of these two demons was to set them against each other. To this end, the villagers dug a large hole on the moors nearby and, knowing that the guytrash so often appeared in conjunction with death, they performed a mock funeral, placing the straw effigy in a coffin at the bottom of the excavation. For the spinning banshee, they laid a trail of honey, corn and salt from the castle to the pit for her to follow.

With this accomplished, they retreated to a safe distance and kept watch as midnight drew near. Sure enough, the guytrash soon came prowling round and disappeared into the pit to inspect the 'corpse'. Only moments thereafter, the ghostly maiden appeared. She bore her spindle as ever, but this time she did not wail and her face bore a look of calm satisfaction. Upon reaching the pit, she began to weave her thread across it and as she did so the guytrash let out a terrible howl, but could not escape. Finally, the walls of the pit collapsed inwards, imprisoning the fiend forever, and the spinning phantom just melted away.

It seems this narrative may have been devised at a relatively late date to tie together two unconnected legends around Goathland – the unusual spinning 'white lady' apparition and the relatively traditional guytrash, both of which were already regarded as portents of tragedy – and provide them with a satisfactory origin story, something often lacked by such traditions. The tale also accounts for an anomalous landscape feature in that area known as the Killing Pits, now thought by archaeologists to be the remains of an ancient settlement or quarry.

This is a process known as 'back-formation' and it may have transformed a number of phantom hounds traditions from ambiguous demonic entities to comprehensible revenants. For instance, a crossroads at Brigham in East Yorkshire, was haunted by 'Willie Sled's dog', supposedly the ghost of a dog that had once belonged to a man who attended the local sandpit. However, as no further legend seems to be attached to it and the crossroads is such a classically liminal location, we may suspect that this belief was laid over an earlier, more ambiguous *genius loci* in the phantom hound mould.

Similarly, the headless hound which haunts the woods around Sheepridge, near Huddersfield, may originally have been the same. To the pre-modern mind, its headlessness needed no explanation. However, by the time the story was properly recorded in 1944, such an uncommon motif required a narrative. Thus, the hound found itself cast as the go-between for two forbidden lovers in the seventeenth century. It would carry messages around its neck from its master at Toothill Hall to the beautiful Sybil Brooke at Newhouse Hall, until one night Sybil's father discovered the ruse and severed the dog's head in a fit of anger. Its decapitated ghost continues to run nightly between the two and in an echo of its former status, portends misfortune to anybody who glimpses it.

Yet, whilst the first wave of folklorists saw the phantom hound as a relic of ancient superstition and the following generation integrated them into conventional ghost lore, there is evidence that the more ambiguous, liminal version of the motif lingers in the collective unconscious. Rumours of such entities have persisted through the twentieth century, with classic sightings recorded at Anston in South Yorkshire, in 1993, and Brackenhill Park in Bradford, in 2002, to name but two examples. Meanwhile, some folklorists have argued that the countless anomalous 'big cat' sightings over the last forty years share a similar epistemological status to encounters with the phantom hound.

It seems that we just cannot let sleeping dogs lie. Much as our efforts to classify the barguest, padfoot, guytrash and skriker are forever doomed to failure by the rich multiplicity of the archaic tradition, attempts to confine the phenomenon to the annals of superstition are similarly frustrated. The phantom hound remains irreducibly liminal, stalking the boundary between fading memory and visceral experience. It is neither one thing nor the other, neither fish nor fowl – but it is that very ambiguity which allows the motif to adapt and endure. Modernity may have destroyed padfoot's traditional harbour, but its brethren prowl the pathways of our imagination still.

EIGHT
TUTELARY SPIRITS

Whilst the phantom hound was typically conceived as inimical to mankind, another class of ambiguous spiritual entity seemed to take a much greater interest in human affairs. Indeed, they were happy not only to exist in close quarters with mortals, but to interact and even cooperate with them. These beings tend to be categorised as 'household spirits' or 'tutelary spirits', however, as with so many folkloric taxonomies, neither term is quite satisfactory. Although in many cases these spirits were associated with a particular household, they were frequently known to haunt outdoor sites as well. Similarly, the word 'tutelary' implies that they acted primarily as a guardian or protector, but whilst this is sometimes true, in English folklore these spirits often present a dual aspect and prove a formidable nuisance for either the household or community to which they are attached.

In Yorkshire, such spirits were known as 'hobs' (with variations such as 'hobthrush') or 'boggarts'. The former seems to have been a more standard appellation in the North and the East of the county, the latter in the South and the West. Generically, they are often classified as 'hobgoblins' or subsumed under the more widely recognised title of 'brownie', which has become an all-purpose term for these spirits in English folklore, despite having originated in the Borders and Scottish lowlands. Nonetheless, there has been some debate about how our ancestors perceived the nature of these entities. Writing in 1802-3, Sir Walter Scott was satisfied that they 'formed a class of beings distinct in habit and disposition from the ... elves (fairies).' However, more recent scholars, such as Katharine Briggs, have chosen to regard them as a species of fairy, albeit one that typically acted individually and preferred to live amongst humans, rather than their own kind.

The most common narratives concerning hobs and boggarts portray them very much as household spirits, closely connected to a particular family or house. Yet they differ from certain tutelary or ancestral spirits in that they are not irrevocably bound to specific people or places. The cooperation they extend to humans is clearly a matter of choice and it can be revoked at any moment, leading the spirit to abandon the family or building forever. They are not like the glaistigs or bean-sidhs of Celtic folklore, fated to serve one dynasty forever. Rather, they come and go on a whim, offering support or creating mischief as they fancy. The capriciousness of such creatures is one of their defining features, and it is never entirely obvious whether their involvement in human affairs was considered a blessing or a curse.

Their representation was also more consistently anthropomorphic than many denizens of the Otherworld, and on the rare occasion hobs or boggarts were actually seen, they were usually described as small, wizened men, naked but for the thick black hair that covered their bodies. Nonetheless, most narratives make clear that it was an uncommon experience to witness these beings in their household capacity. In some cases they were literally invisible, but more often it seems that they were merely very shy and preferred to conduct their business at night, away from prying eyes. That business usually consisted of all the least gratifying farm and household chores, such as sweeping, churning, spinning, weaving, winnowing, threshing and so forth. In return, the hob or boggart usually asked for nothing more than a bowl of milk, to be left out every night on the hearth.

The model spirit in this regard seems to have been the hob that resided for many generations at Hart Hall at Glaisdale on the North York Moors. The Reverend J.C. Atkinson, an avid nineteenth-century folklore collector who served for many decades as the vicar of nearby Danby, noted,

> In the barn, if there was a weight of work craving to be done and time was scant or force insufficient, Hob would come unasked to the rescue. Unaccountable strength seemed to be the chief attribute ascribed to him ... What mortal strength was clearly incapable of, that was the work which Hob took upon himself ... There was no reminiscence of his mischievousness, harmless malice or even tricksiness. He was not of those who ... resent the possibly unintended interference with elfish prerogative.

Yet despite this spirit's evidently placid disposition, Hob left Hart Hall in high dudgeon, as was the case with so many of his kind. The story was told that one night the master of the house happened to catch sight of Hob about his work in the barn, and noticed that through all the creature's labour he was as naked as sin. The master concluded that to reward the industrious hob for his patient toil, he would provide it with a Harding smock, much like the other household servants wore. It was placed out for the creature on the hearth overnight and the master hid himself nearby to observe its gratitude. However, Hob was not impressed at all – after examining the clothes, he was heard to remark,

Hart Hall in Glaisdale, home to a famous hob. (Kai Roberts)

Gin Hob mun hae nowght but a Hardin' hamp
He'll come nae mair nowther to berry nor stamp.

And with these words he abandoned Hart Hall, never to return.

Although this tale in relation to Hart Hall is one of the most famous concerning hobs in the canon of Yorkshire folklore, it is far from unique. A similar narrative is told at several other locations in the county. The boggart of Sturfit Hall at Reeth in Wensleydale left the house for exactly the same reason, whilst the boggart of Close House near Addingham in Craven was offended by the gift of a red cap, and in a novel twist, the hob attached to the Oughtred family at Upleatham departed when a farmhand forgetfully left his coat hanging on the winnowing machine overnight, which the creature then believed had been placed there as an offering for him. In all cases the essence of the story is the same: a hob or boggart would take umbrage at any attempt to present him with clothes, and forsake the house and family for good.

This tale is not only common in Yorkshire; it is well known in relation to household spirits throughout England and the Scottish lowlands. A similar narrative was recorded concerning an unnamed demon as early as the fourteenth century by the preacher John of Promyard; then again in connection with brownies by Reginald Scot in his influential treatise of 1584, *The Discoverie of Witchcraft*; and once again about Puck in an influential sixteenth-century chapbook, *The Mad Pranks and Merry Jests of Robin Goodfellow* (which famously influenced William Shakespeare's *A Midsummer Night's Dream*). In recent years, it has been incorporated in J.K. Rowling's Harry Potter mythos as a trait of house-elves, meaning the motif will remain familiar to children for generations to come, albeit in a consciously fictional context.

The moral of the story is somewhat uncertain and regional variations make it difficult to identify a single theme. For instance, in the case of the Hob of Hart Hall the phrasing of the rhyme suggests that he was offended by the paucity of the offering. He indicates that he believes he deserves better than a mere Harding smock. However, in other versions, it seems to be the very notion of being rewarded for his work at all that provokes the household spirit. Writing in 1856, George Henderson suggests that such spirits were regarded as 'commissioned by God to relieve mankind under the drudgery of original sin, hence they were forbidden to accept wages or bribes.' However, this seems unlikely given that Christianity and the belief in household spirits generally stood in tension with each other.

It seems more likely that it is another expression of the hob or boggart's fierce individuality and free will. Hilda Ellis Davidson notes, 'It is clear in the Icelandic tales that the guardian spirits made a contract with the farmers they chose to help, but they could never be regarded as servants. They were the luck-bringers and the luck must be freely given.' A functionalist approach might cynically speculate that the story impressed on the rural labouring classes the virtue of treating work as its own reward. It implied that the servant should be happy to do all the sweeping, and the farmhand should be content to get on with the threshing without any expectation of advantage – certain *other* creatures were thus satisfied and why should human ingrates think any differently? Conversely, it may be taken to indicate that hard work *would* be rewarded and the recipients should be appropriately thankful for their master's largesse.

Yet, whilst this story indicates that, should a family wish to rid themselves of their hob or boggart, all that was required was to leave it a gift of clothes, a seemingly contradictory strand of the household spirit tradition suggests that an unwanted hob or boggart was almost impossible to dislodge. Unlike the blameless Hob of Hart Hall, many such beings had a dual aspect which ranged from trivial acts of mischief to outright malice. It seems that household spirits were particularly sensitive creatures and would take offence at a variety of perceived slights, such as general mockery, criticism of its work, interference with its movements, failure to leave a bowl of milk for it to drink or spying on its labours. Some writers have suggested that when a hob was angered it *became* a boggart, and it is true that 'boggart' seems to be applied to mischievous household spirits more often than helpful ones, but in other cases the terms are used inconsistently or interchangeably.

In some instances, such as at Spaldington Hall in the East Riding, the boggart's shenanigans would be little more than a harmless irritation. Robin Round-Cap – as this example was known – gained fame for 'remixing the winnowed wheat with the chaff ... putting out the fire ... kicking over the milk-pail.' In this respect, he seems to have acted as a scapegoat for all the minor irritations of daily life, not to mention a phenomenon on to which clumsy and lazy servants could deflect blame for their lapses. In other cases, however, the spirit's devilry was more pronounced and less explicable. Katharine Briggs writes, 'The traditional behaviour of boggarts and mischievous hobgoblins is indistinguishable from what psychical researchers call "poltergeist manifestations" ... The phenomena are fairly constant. There is always knocking, almost always the throwing of stones and pebbles, over-setting of dishes, sometimes throwing of fire [and] clattering of china.'

On other occasions, the boggart became a great deal more violent. A story collected from a Yorkshire tailor in the 1750s relates,

> The children's bread and butter would be snatched away, or their porringers of bread and milk would be dashed down by an invisible hand ... One day the farmer's youngest boy was playing with the shoe-horn and as children will do he stuck the horn in a knot-hole ... The horn darted out with velocity and struck the poor child over the head.

Meanwhile, a story recorded around Whitby in 1828 suggests that one farm hob took umbrage when the farmer's new wife cut back on household expenditure and replaced the cream regularly left out for him overnight with skimmed milk. The offended hob not only stopped performing the household chores, but it began to make strange noises and tear the covers from the bed in the middle of the night, and even killed the poultry.

Houses which had a reputation for 'poltergeist'-style hauntings (prior to the first use of this German loanword in an English context by the Society for Psychical Research in the late nineteenth century) were frequently known colloquially as 'boggart houses'. Several examples are found in West Yorkshire, including at Midgley, Brighouse and Leeds, where a whole council estate has inherited the name from the now-demolished house on whose site it stands. It was famously applied to Bierley Hall near Cleckheaton sometime in the early 1800s, when the manifestations in one upstairs room of the building grew so violent that crowds of people gathered outside hoping to glimpse the phenomena, whilst numerous attempts were made to exorcise the room by clergyman and cunning folk, but all to no avail.

If the hob or boggart began to behave in such a fashion, it also became notoriously difficult to get rid of. In a story which rivals the narrative of the gifting of clothes for its ubiquity and geographical spread, the spirit becomes so troublesome and tenacious that the family decides to move house and leave it behind. To this end, they quietly pack up all their belongings onto a cart and creep out of their former home early one morning. When they are only a short distance down the road, a neighbour sees them and enquires as to what is happening, to which the voice of the boggart responds from the cart, 'We're flitting!' The family abandon their flight and return to their old home, resigned to the fact that if they are going to be harassed, they might as well be harassed in familiar surroundings.

This is another classic example of a migratory legend, which is told about different locations across Yorkshire from the Holderness coast, to Cliviger on the Lancashire border – not to mention several neighbouring counties. It is now impossible to tell exactly where the narrative originated from, but despite its frequent appearance in collections of the county's folklore today, Reverend J.C. Atkinson for one doubted that it originated in Yorkshire. However much the boggart stubbornly refuses to be evicted, Atkinson suggests that any Yorkshireman is more stubborn still and would not be driven from his home by a mere spirit. From his extensive forty years' experience as vicar of Danby, he notes that, 'Flitting is, like matrimony, "not to be lightly or wantonly taken in hand"; and, still less, abandoned after the said fashion.'

Nonetheless, the tale colourfully makes the point that ridding your family of a troublesome boggart was not an easy prospect. At one time they were evidently considered such a nuisance around Yeadon in West Yorkshire, that the town accounts actually record sums paid from the public purse for 'boggart-catching'! In many stories, priests or cunning folk have to be called in and they must resort to imaginative tactics to succeed. Whilst the clergy were unable to exorcise Bierley Hall's resident spook, in other places intervention proved more effective. For instance, the prayers of three men of the cloth succeeded in coaxing Robin Round-Cap from Spaldington Hall into the confines of a nearby well, where he was condemned to remain for a certain number of years.

The prolific nineteenth-century Yorkshire antiquarian, Harry Speight, suggested that it was the hobs and boggarts who had been forced to leave their homes – whether through taking offence or compulsion – that subsequently became an even greater nuisance to unwary travellers in the wild. Following its departure from Close House, he suggests the boggart has 'ever since been wandering through the dale and field, an idle worthless wight, no good to anyone and tempting others to

Hob Holes at Runswick Bay, home to a malevolent hob. (Kai Roberts)

idle, evil ways.' Whilst no folk narrative makes this trajectory clear itself, the notion nicely accounts for the seeming disparity between relatively well-behaved domestic hobs or boggarts (such as Hob of Hart Hall) and the less-civilised, more naturally malignant examples which roamed the countryside.

The hob that gave its name to Hob Hole, a large sea cave in Runswick Bay on the North Yorkshire coast, retained some vestige of its former generosity. In less enlightened times, local mothers took their children there at low tide to beg a cure for whooping cough, invoking the spirit with the words,

> Hob Hole hob, my bairn's gotten t'kin cough
> Tak 't off, Tak 't off!

However, one source adds that when the hob was not remedying common childhood illnesses, he 'used to wander over the moors behind the bay with a lantern and often decoyed travellers into the pots to be found amongst the rock or else in a driving night storm of rain would offer them shelter in his hole and leave them to perish by the incoming tide.'

Hobs and boggarts in the wild were often associated with caves and potholes. In 'The Boggart of Hellen Pot', Victorian folklorist Sabine Baring-Gould narrates a first-hand account in which he finds himself lost at night in the limestone country between Pen-y-ghent and Arncliffe – an area riddled with such chasms. Stumbling blindly across the moors, he encounters a lame man, who, despite never speaking, seems to be leading him to safety. Baring-Gould notes 'The impression forced itself on me that just thus would a man walk who had his neck and legs broken ...' But after taking him some distance along the bed of a stream, the strange man vanishes, leaving the unwary traveller to stagger on in the darkness. Then, suddenly he reappears, just as his victim is teetering on the edge of Hull Pot – a vast, gaping rent in the fabric of the landscape – and tries to drag him down. Baring-Gould only saves himself by clinging to a rowan tree which overhung the precipice.

Baring-Gould was a notorious romanticist and it seems unlikely that he was recounting an incident that he actually experienced personally. However, it probably does record a narrative that was popular in the Three

Hurtle Pot near Chapel-le-Dale, home to a malevolent boggart. (Kathryn Wilson)

Peaks region of Ribblesdale in the nineteenth century. At Hurtle Pot, a pothole near Chapel-le-Dale in the same area, a boggart was once believed to pull unfortunate passers-by down into the hole and drown them in the murky depths. A local writer remarks, 'Both this and Jingle Pot are choked with water from subterranean channels in flood time and then there is heard such an intermittent throbbing, gurgling noise, accompanied by what seems dismal gaspings, that a timorous listener might easily believe the boggart was drowning his victims.'

Meanwhile, in the lead mining district around Grassington and Greenhow Hill, the miners had their own tutelary spirits with a similar dual nature to hobs and boggarts. Locally they were known as the Ghostly Shift, but miners who had migrated to Yorkshire from Cornwall brought with them their own term – the 'Knockers'. These spirits were so-called due to their tendency to make mysterious, loud rapping noises, especially in new workings. In some cases, the miners believed these sounds to be a sign that they were nearing a rich seam; in other instances, however, they were regarded as portents of disaster and thought to occur just before any serious accident. Often in those cases, superstition amongst the miners was such that they refused to continue work until further safety precautions had been taken.

The association between such beings and chthonic regions suggests some relation to the ancestors. The Knockers or Ghostly Shift were quite explicitly regarded as the personification of all the miners who had died in shaft falls over the generations, but whilst in the case of household or other tutelary spirits the connection with the dead is not so unequivocal, such correspondences suggest that hobs and boggarts may be a corrupted remembrance of the ancestral spirits that are a common tradition across many non-monotheistic world views. Although the Victorian conceit that all folklore is a fossilised relic of pre-Christian pagan practices has largely been discredited, it is nonetheless possible to draw valuable parallels with beliefs in other pre-modern cultures, as long as they are not overstated.

The Roman 'Lares' are the most notable example in this respect. Classical literature indicates that these benign household spirits were believed to be the personification of all the ancestors who had been buried beneath the house, or the foundation sacrifice offered when the structure was built – both common practices in pre-modern societies. The correspondence between the Lares and British household, or tutelary, spirits was observed as early as 1605, by Pierre de Loyer in his *Treatise of Spectres or Strange Sights, Visions and Apparitions appearing sensibly unto Men*, and it is not unreasonable to suggest that hobs and boggarts were descended from a similar tradition, as there is evidence that both household burial and foundation sacrifice were practised by some of the pre-Christian cultures of this country.

If the connection with caves – often regarded as liminal points and entrance portals to the underworld – is not sufficient to establish a relation between household and ancestral spirits, then it should be noted that we also find hobs and boggarts associated with the material remnants of ancient cultures. In Farndale, on the North York Moors, a hob notoriously haunted a prominent prehistoric burial cairn known as Obtrush Roque. Meanwhile, Lile Hob of Blea Moor seemed to guard a treasure of obscure antiquity. It haunted the moorland road between Newby Head and Gearstones, and was known for jumping onto passing carts in the dark and hitching a short ride before vanishing again. However, the hob apparently disappeared for good after a Dentdale farmer discovered 'three armlets made of silver, inlaid with enamel' on the moor and removed them to give to the landowner.

The road across Blea Moor, haunt of a treasure guarding hob. (Kathryn Wilson)

By the nineteenth century, when the majority of Yorkshire traditions concerning hobs and boggarts were recorded, it is likely that their origin as ancestral spirits had long since been consciously forgotten and only a vague, intuitive remembrance endured. As Katharine Briggs notes, unlike the Roman *Lares* and other household spirits of antiquity, British examples were not irrevocably tied to a particular building but seemed to come and go as they chose, conspicuously exercising their free will in the matter. Perhaps most significantly, however, they were no longer exclusively helpful guardian spirits, but had acquired their characteristic dual nature.

One hypothesis as to how this capricious and malevolent side had entered the household spirit tradition in Britain, is that it was a consequence of the Protestant Reformation in the sixteenth century. It seems likely that a belief in beneficial household spirits endured through the Middle Ages because, as Hilda Ellis Davidson notes, 'After Christianity was set up, many concepts on a simple level, like those of the household guardian spirits, persisted because they were humble enough to escape condemnation, and also because they held a strong appeal for young and old.' However, whilst Catholicism could comfortably live side-by-side with belief in such spirits because it was not a threat to their overall cosmology, this was not the case for Protestantism and especially not Puritanism.

Following the Reformation, theologians in England were especially keen to discourage any of the characteristically Catholic beliefs which they had so decisively rejected. Amongst them was the concept of Purgatory – a realm in which minor sinners were held and purified before being granted entrance to Heaven. For Catholics, earthbound spirits were souls who were unable to proceed straight to Heaven and existed in a purgatorial state. But because Protestants rejected the reality of Purgatory, it followed that they must also reject the reality of earthbound spirits. Accordingly, whilst they did not go as far as to deny that people *thought* they encountered such spirits, they redefined them as demons in disguise, and throughout the sixteenth and seventeenth centuries, Protestant polemicists churned out numerous tracts denouncing them.

It was, perhaps, this process of transformation that causes Katharine Briggs to observe, 'The line between the devil and the hobgoblin is very lightly drawn. Often the same story is told about both, they behave in the same manner, and the same methods are necessary in dealing with them.' However, whilst the notion of household spirits as demons eventually entered the collective consciousness, it seems that folk tradition also stubbornly cleaved to an older belief in their beneficence, no matter how contradictory that might seem. It is likely that this was especially true in the remoter areas of the northern counties of England, where vestiges of Catholicism clung on more tenaciously; and whilst we should always be wary of such neat explanations in folklore, this process may account for the dual nature ascribed to hobs and boggarts in Yorkshire.

In some instances, however, it is clear that such beings were conceived of primarily as demons. As previously noted, the term 'boggart' is more often applied to mischievous and downright vindictive tutelary spirits than 'hob', although it is not clear to what extent this was true of the folk tradition itself and to what extent it was the result of collectors' artificial taxonomies. Nonetheless, some writers have suggested a putative linguistic root between the words 'boggart' and 'bogeyman' – a generic label applied to 'any figure deliberately used to frighten others, almost always children, to control their behaviour.'

It is clear that some boggarts were conceived in such a fashion. For instance, the boggart that haunted Wibsey Slack near Bradford was described as 'an exceedingly tall man with gigantic feet. His footfalls, which have been compared to the head of a steam-hammer, were said to reverberate through the whole neighbourhood.' In the nineteenth century, Wibsey Slack was a 'dreary stretch of bleak windswept waste' and precisely the sort of place parents would discourage their children from going. The boggart of Bunting Nook near Sheffield seems to have performed a similar function. Bunting Nook was renowned as a desolate place, even in the twentieth century, and the noted Victorian folklorist S.O. Addy remarks that this boggart was 'held up as a terror to children'.

Elsewhere, we find unique baleful tutelary spirits such as 'Awd Goggie, who in the East Riding was said to haunt orchards, presumably in an effort to keep children from scrumping apples. Similarly, in Craven there is Churn Milk Peg, 'a fearsome hag, whose only business in life apart from smoking a very dainty fairy-pipe, was to scare children when they bent on plucking unripe fruit from the hedgerow ... If the bairns were rash enough to disregard the warning, Churn Milk Peg carried them off forthwith to some dim abode where sun never shone and stars never twinkled.'

At Flamborough on the Holderness coast, a dangerous pit was reputedly the abode of Jenny Gallows and if a person circled the hollow a certain number of times, she would rise up and cry out:

Ah'll tee on me bonnet
An' put on me shoe
An' if thoo's not off
Ah'll suan catch thoo!

According to local legend, a farmer once attempted the feat on horseback, whereupon Jenny Gallows appeared and pursued the reckless rider as far as the boundary of the village. She did not seem able to follow him beyond its threshold, but before he got away, 'She bit a piece clean out of the horse's flank and the old mare had a white patch there to her dying day.'

Every environment seems to have possessed its own characteristic bogeyman. The wild uplands of the Yorkshire Dales were haunted by the Brown Man of the Moors, described as a 'dwarf, big-headed, wide of shoulders, with a shock of tousled hair and clothes russet as October's brackens. He lies in wait for every traveller, challenging him to combat.' Meanwhile, the urban streets of South Yorkshire were terrorised by a monster known as Jack-In-Irons. With some similarities to the Wibsey boggart, this entity was imagined as 'a terribly strong man, gaunt, and at least ten feet high, with clanking chains at feet and wrists. He suddenly appears in quiet streets, or springs out of dark corners, in order to carry off the unwary pedestrian to unknown regions.'

As Steve Roud and Jacqueline Simpson cannily note, a bogeyman is 'often the final function of a belief adults no longer share.' This is certainly true of the hob and boggart today. Whilst the terms endure in toponyms and regional folk tale collections, it is now rarely used with any sincerity. Poltergeists have succeeded the idea of the malevolent boggart and are the province of parapsychological investigators, whilst the classic household spirit itself is relegated to the realm of children's books and tourist lore. However, it is clear that they once represented an active, vibrant tradition across Yorkshire, stretching back many centuries. As J.C. Atkinson observed of one of his informants, '[She] told forth her tale as of things that had happened under everybody's cognisance, and as might be only the other day; and of which she had only just missed personal cognisance herself by coming a little too late on the scene.'

NINE

GHOSTS

In view of the variety of supernatural phenomena already covered in this book, there are at least two good reasons why the reader may ask why ghosts deserve a chapter to themselves. Firstly, to what extent do ghosts qualify as folklore? As the existence of such phenomena remains a moot point – in a recent survey, 38 per cent of the British population affirmed their belief in ghosts and 19 per cent claimed to have encountered one – it could be argued that to baldly define such belief as 'folklore' is begging the question. Accordingly, this chapter will only consider historical and 'legendary' ghosts – i.e. those spectres which exist as rumour alone – rather than first-hand accounts or memorates. Such an approach will illustrate how popular beliefs about ghosts have changed over the centuries to reflect the dominant religious, philosophical and cultural concerns of their age.

The second issue is whether it is fair to demarcate 'ghosts' as a class of phenomena distinct from the other supernatural entities in this book: is it possible to say, for instance, that a ghost is something different from a guytrash or boggart? It is true that such taxonomies may be rather arbitrary and imprecise. As Jacqueline Simpson notes, 'Psychologically, any experience of the uncanny is understood through the belief system of the perceiver and his/her community. It may be experienced as an encounter with a ghost, a fairy, a demon or an alien from outer space – whatever seems plausible at that time and place.' However, broadly speaking, a ghost can be characterised as the spirit of a potentially identifiable deceased individual that has returned to walk the material world, and this chapter will discuss belief that conforms to such a definition.

It can be argued that belief in ghosts as we understand them today arose in England around the thirteenth century, when the concept of Purgatory became

Byland Abbey in North Yorkshire, where the earliest ghosts in the county were recorded.
(Kai Roberts)

orthodox theological doctrine. Prior to this point, the restless dead had typically
been characterised as revenants – i.e. animated corpses possessed by the Devil,
more closely resembling our modern idea of vampires or zombies. Writing around
1198, the Yorkshire monk William of Newburgh documents several examples of
such belief in the county. Yet, approximately two centuries later, a collection of
anecdotes concerning encounters with the dead, recorded by an anonymous monk
of Byland Abbey, reveals tales of revenants to have been overtaken by narratives
featuring visible but incorporeal spirits. Whilst these are credited with more agency
than many ghosts, they are clear forerunners of the modern spectre.

The notion of Purgatory as an intermediate realm in which the souls of minor
sinners were purified before they could be received into Heaven, provided a
conceptual framework by which the spirit of a departed individual could return to
this world. Invariably, such spirits manifested to demand post-mortem absolution
of sin and intercessory prayers, which could hasten the progress of a soul through
Purgatory. A number of the stories recorded by the Byland monk ably illustrate
this doctrine and it is thought they may have been preserved for use as exemplar in
sermons, emphasising the importance of regular shriving and intercessory prayer in
terms which an uneducated congregation might understand.

For instance, one story concerns the ghost of a monk of Newburgh Priory who
during his life had been excommunicated for stealing some silver spoons. His spirit
appeared to a ploughman and begged him to retrieve the spoons from where they
had been hidden, take them to the Prior of Newburgh and ask him to absolve

the monk's sin. The ploughman followed these instructions and the ghost was able to rest in peace. Another tale involves an Ampleforth woman who had unjustly bequeathed her property to her brother instead of her husband and children, who had been evicted after her death. The woman's ghost appeared to a local man and requested that he beseech her brother to give the land to her husband and sons, or else she could not rest. Her brother refused, so the woman appeared to him herself and told him that he too would know no peace when he died.

As we can see from these examples, the attributes of ghosts during the Middle Ages were quite different from later specimens. Although their initial appearance might cause alarm, their behaviour was often humble and rarely malevolent; they appeared during the hours of daylight as much as at night, and in everyday places such as a field during ploughing; and, perhaps most unusually, they were able to communicate and effectively articulate the reason they were condemned to walk the earth. Whilst returning spirits might be feared, they were not in themselves a negative force: such restlessness was unfortunate for the spirit concerned, but it was still regarded as a natural aspect of Creation rather than a transgression against the proper order.

All this changed with the Reformation. Protestant theology rejected the doctrine of Purgatory and saintly intercession as Popish superstition, meaning intercessory prayer was no longer required by the dead. It followed that spirits could not return to seek such favours from the living. The soul was either comfortably ensconced in Heaven or condemned to the eternal torments of Hell, and there was no way back from either. However, popular belief in apparitions of the dead was stubborn and sightings of such phenomena persisted. Reformed theology was forced to account for this evidence and it did so by suggesting that ghosts were not the spirits of the departed, but visions of angels or more frequently, demons masquerading as the dead. It is with this development that ghosts began to be perceived as baleful aberrations and more profoundly feared.

Yet although this belief was acceptable to the more Puritanical – indeed, the frequency of ghost sightings may have further confirmed their belief in the Devil's growing power on Earth – many Protestants continued to argue over the precise nature of ghosts. Given the obstinacy of such reports and their association with spirits of the dead, it seemed that to deny the possibility that ghosts were restless souls was to risk denying the afterlife. With the rise in a purely materialist ontology and rationalist religion fostered by the philosophical writings of Rene Descartes, the threat of Sadduceeism (the denial of the afterlife) became a considerable cause for concern during the seventeenth century. Protestants began to endorse belief in ghosts once more; as proof of the immortality of the soul and a counter-argument to sceptical philosophy.

However, the purposes of ghosts underwent revision. Rather than embodying a theological message, their concerns became secular: they appeared by divine providence in order to right wrongs, prevent future injustice, correct immoral

The room in Bolling Hall near Bradford, where the Earl of Newcastle witnessed a terrifying apparition. (Kai Roberts)

behaviour and so forth. In Yorkshire, there is a fine illustration of ghosts' new rationale in the story of the apparition that appeared to the Earl of Newcastle, at Bolling Hall in Bradford during the Civil Wars. A Royalist army under the earl had laid siege to the city which was occupied by Parliamentarians; they had been bombarding it constantly with cannons and the earl declared that he would put the whole citizenry to the sword. But the night before he was due to carry out his threat, he awoke in his room at Bolling Hall to see the apparition of a white lady standing at the foot of the bed. He looked on in terror as it pulled his bedclothes aside and uttered, 'Pity poor Bradford! Pity poor Bradford!' The following morning, the earl spared the city.

In this period, it was such an article of faith that murder victims could appear as ghosts to expose the crime against them, that magistrates accepted testimony of such sightings as evidence. For instance, on 14 April 1690, William Barwick murdered his pregnant wife Mary whilst they were walking near Cawood Castle and buried her body beside a pool in that region, a crime for which he was tried and executed on 16 September of that year at the York Assizes. The case was remarkable in that Barwick's offence had seemingly come to light through supernatural intervention detailed in the statement of his brother-in-law, Thomas Lofthouse, and as such was recorded by the antiquarian John Aubrey in his 1696 book, *Miscellanies*, as evidence of the existence of ghosts.

Lofthouse had asserted that on the day of the murder, Barwick had told him that Mary was staying with relatives at Selby. However, around noon a few days later, Lofthouse was drawing water from that pool when he witnessed a female apparition walking in front of him. She looked and was dressed much like his wife's sister, but she was unnaturally pale. After a while she sat down at a spot near the pool and held 'something like a white bag' in her lap – perhaps suggestive of a swaddled baby, representing her unborn child. Lofthouse told his wife what he witnessed from which she concluded that her sister had been murdered and buried where her ghost had been seen. They searched for her at the relatives' house in Selby, but when she could not be found they applied to the Lord Mayor of York for Barwick's arrest.

These cases became increasingly rare as the Enlightenment gathered pace through the eighteenth century and educated opinion turned firmly against the possibility of ghosts. Yet, much as the Reformation had failed to extinguish such belief two centuries earlier, it persisted amongst the majority of the population. Nonetheless, without a dominant religious or moral agenda which could provide a function for their existence, ghost traditions grew fractured, contradictory and confused. Moreover, the apparitions themselves became increasingly purposeless: they no longer manifested to seek absolution or intercession, nor to expose crimes or prevent injustice. Often, they simply haunted a specified location and terrified residents or travellers, but otherwise rarely had any influence over mortal affairs.

A vast majority of the enigmatic headless horsemen and white ladies which fill up so many Victorian topography and folklore collections, seem to owe their existence to that stripping away of religious and moral function of ghosts which had been accomplished by the late eighteenth and early nineteenth century. Yorkshire has no shortage of such spectres. The popularity of headless ghosts is especially puzzling and they are so abundant in the county that it would be a tedious, perhaps impossible, task to list them all. Suffice it to say, nearly every locality had such a ghost, which would walk or ride nightly for no obvious reason. However, they exist primarily as rumour legends, and few first-hand accounts of encounters with these apparitions exist.

Some traditions were more colourful than others: a headless woman that haunted the road between Leven and Riston in East Yorkshire used to leap up behind horsemen and slap their ears, whilst at Stokesley, just such a ghost in burning clothes was said to walk from Lady Cross to Kirby Lane, then disappear with a shriek. At Low Hall in Yeadon another headless woman emerged from the oak panelling of a bedchamber and glided across it, white robe flowing behind her, to disappear into a concealed chamber by the fireplace. Yet another example haunted a barn at Dalton near Thirsk, and appeared carrying her head like a lantern, emitting light from its eyes, nostrils and mouth. There was a hole in the barn wall supposedly made by a horrified tramp as he tried to escape from this vision, and it was shown to visitors as a mark of the tradition's authenticity.

The tomb of Sir Richard Beaumont, whose headless phantom walks nearby. (Kai Roberts)

The headless state of such ghosts is perplexing. Had the ghost represented a known individual who had been beheaded it would make sense, but decapitation was actually a rare mode of execution in English history, reserved for the aristocracy. Sometimes the condition of the ghost is associated with mere head injury, such as the headless apparition that haunts the foot of Colburn Nab in Staithes, identified with a girl whose skull was shattered by a falling rock from the cliff above. In other instances a vague tradition seems to have been invented to account for the appearance. For instance, natives of Linthwaite claimed that the headless horseman who rode the lanes in those parts was the ghost of a local chief who had been beheaded on orders of the king for his disloyalty, although the historical record is silent about such an individual.

Perhaps more egregiously, the headless ghost of Sir Richard Beaumont, said to walk between Kirkheaton and Lepton near Huddersfield on the night of 5 July, was supposed to have been decapitated in a quarrel with a fellow highwayman over their spoils. This is despite the fact Sir Richard is known to have died in 1631 of natural causes and there is no evidence to suggest that he ever engaged in criminal activity. It seems likely that Sir Richard's ghost was originally headless for some symbolic reason which was forgotten by subsequent generations, and the story about his death was appended when an explanation was demanded; or the phantom was once an anonymous headless ghost onto whom Sir Richard's name was superimposed by later tradition.

Conversely, when the apparition of an historical figure who actually was beheaded is seen, the condition of being headless was not observed! This is true of the ghost of Richard le Scrope, a medieval Archbishop of York, who was executed for treason by order of Henry IV on 29 May 1405 in a field outside the walls of the city. Locals believed that Scrope's ghost occasionally appeared conducting his own phantom funeral, which processed from his former palace at Bishopthorpe to the scene of his execution. An apparition assumed to be Scrope on account of his attire was supposed to walk behind a floating coffin; his head was not only intact, but bent over the pages of a large book from which he read, although no sound issued from his mouth.

A similar nebulousness prevails in the case of white ladies. Numerous sites in the county are haunted by white ladies who seem to walk for the most ill-defined reasons. The remains of a fortified manor house at Hall Garth in Wetherby were thought to be frequented by such an apparition, connected with some unspoken tragedy in a family who had once dwelt there. Similarly, the vicinity of a cliff just outside Barwick-in-Elmet was haunted by a female phantom dressed in white, who appeared to wash her garments in the beck near Ass Bridge. She was supposed to be the spirit of a woman murdered at Parlington but no further information was given and it is unclear whether such a crime ever took place.

Some folklorists have suggested that white ladies are actually a degraded relic of fairy belief, and are not so much spectres but genius loci whose original tradition evolved into something more appropriate for the age. It is certainly true that such apparitions tend to haunt archetypally liminal sites of the sort often associated with fairies; for instance, watery places and bridges as can be seen in the case of the Barwick 'cliff lady'. White ladies are also regularly linked with ancient ruins and earthworks; perhaps most famously in the example of the White Lady of Skipsea Castle, in which the shade of a beautiful young woman wearing a white robe mournfully wanders the remains of a Norman motte-and-bailey castle. Another white lady haunts Danes Dyke, a two-mile long defensive earthwork of Iron-Age provenance near Flamborough.

It was also during the eighteenth century that the motif of evil men and tragic death became strongly associated with ghosts. As the folklorist Gillian Bennett observes, whilst the dead no longer seemed to return for any purpose, the popular dislike of ambiguity meant that such phenomena required a *cause*. Bennett writes, 'If their actions *after* death have no logic, it follows that any rationale must be found in events *before* their death. The havoc they wreak after their death therefore gets explained by the havoc of their life or dying. Either they are assumed to have had a malice so intense that it cannot die, or they are assumed to have had a death so cruel that the death itself cannot die and goes on being re-enacted somehow.'

This is best exemplified in the haunting of Calverley Hall near Bradford, scene of one of the most infamous tragedies in the history of the county. Sir Walter Calverley, owner of the hall in the late sixteenth and early seventeenth century, had married

The earthworks at Skipsea Castle, haunted by a white lady. (Kai Roberts)

Philippa Brook, the daughter of Lord Cobham; but whilst Philippa was a virtuous woman, Sir Walter was a wild and dissolute man. On 23 April 1604, heavily in debt to his creditors and possessed by a drunken rage, Sir Walter attempted to murder his wife and succeeded in killing two of his children. He was caught as he attempted to flee on horseback and after refusing to plead at his trial, he was sentenced to 'peine forte et dure' – a form of torture-cum-execution in which heavy stones were piled on the defendant's chest until he either entered a plea or expired from suffocation.

Sir Walter persisted in his refusal to cooperate and towards the end was said to have cried to a faithful servant who had remained by his side, 'Them that love Sir Walter, pile on! pile on!' His apparition is said to have endlessly repeated those words as he wandered the lane which runs to Calverly Hall. Alternatively, his ghost rode a headless steed and took great delight in hunting down unwary travellers, until he became such a menace that the local community had him exorcised. Meanwhile, inside the hall, a permanent bloodstain is supposed to discolour the woodwork in the chamber where the murder was committed, a stain which no amount of scrubbing can remove – another common motif in ghost lore of this kind.

Sometimes the sin need not be as mortal as murder. The man who built Swinsty Hall in Washburndale made his fortune by looting the houses of dead men in London during the Great Plague of 1665, and locals believed his apparition could be seen obsessively washing coins in the Greenwell at Timble in an attempt to disinfect them. The headless ghost of Sir Josceline Percy was believed to drive four headless horses around the streets of Beverley night after night, for the crime of once entering Beverley Minster on horseback. Even mere eccentricity became

Calverley Hall in West Yorkshire, where the ghost of murderous Sir Walter still walks.
(Kai Roberts)

enough to justify supernatural immortality. As the folklorist Christina Hole notes,
it reflected 'the popular inability to believe that so strong a personality could really
have suffered the common fate of death.'

It was not just the sinners who were thought to return: often the sinned
against suffered a similar fate in death and as we have seen with headless ghosts
and white ladies, such was the connection in the popular mind between tragedy
and subsequent hauntings that all manner of apocryphal traditions were devised
to account for a phantom's appearance, or they were often conflated with other
popular local legends. For instance, the White Lady of Skipsea Castle is frequently
said to embody the wife of the castle's builder, Drogo de Bevere, who fought at the
Battle of Hastings with William the Conqueror. For his loyalty he was gifted the
lands of Holderness, along with the hand of William's niece in marriage. However,
their match was not successful and Drogo is said to have poisoned the unfortunate
girl before fleeing back to Normandy.

Arguing against the genuine identification of the White Lady of Skipsea Castle as
the unfortunate Lady de Bevere is the suspicion that the tradition of her murder is
apocryphal and may be entirely fictitious. This is compounded by the curious but
undeniable fact that historical phantoms were never seen until the late seventeenth
century, and then did not appear in any great number until the nineteenth. The
ghosts of the medieval and early modern period are always those of the recently

dead; spirits from the distant past are not recorded until the advent of compulsory education and particularly the teaching of history. This may explain why ghosts are so associated with major conflicts which left a deep scar on the psyche of the region – or more prosaically, were well known from the history books.

In Yorkshire, this invariably means the Reformation or the English Civil Wars. A phantom known as the White Lass of North Kilvington once haunted Borrowby Bridge over the Spittlebeck, and was identified with the daughter of the Meynells. Tradition asserted that the girl had been raped and murdered by Henry VIII's commissioners, when her staunchly Catholic family had refused to cooperate with the confiscation of monastic assets. Meanwhile, the headless woman that haunts a bedchamber at Watton Abbey is supposed to be the ghost of a former Royalist owner, murdered in that room by Roundhead irregulars as they looted the area following the Parliamentarian victory at Marston Moor. The story claims they beheaded her, but we have already seen how deceptive that motif can be.

Similarly, there is perhaps no reason beyond the romanticising power of tradition why the ghostly ladies believed to haunt Nappa Hall in Wensleydale and Manor Lodge in Sheffield should be identified with Mary, Queen of Scots. The unfortunate cousin of Elizabeth I passed only two nights at Nappa Hall as a guest of the Metcalfe family, whilst she was imprisoned at nearby Castle Bolton between July 1568 and January 1569. Although a maid some two centuries later claimed to have seen a spectre answering Mary's description at Nappa Hall, she was not executed until 1587 at Fotheringay Castle in Northamptonshire and there seems little reason why her ghost should return to that hall in particular. Equally, she only spent brief periods at

Nappa Hall in Wensleydale, haunted by the ghost of Mary Queen of Scots? (Kai Roberts)

Manor Lodge between 1570 and 1584, whilst moving between various properties as a prisoner of the Earl of Shrewsbury. Still, her ghost is rumoured to haunt the roof of the Turret House – the only surviving part of the building.

The connection between unnatural, tragic death and hauntings was so firmly established in the collective psyche that Mary was an inevitable candidate for post-mortem return, no matter how tenuous her connection with a property might have been. However, it was not just unnatural death which guaranteed such a fate: improper burial had similar consequences. These traditions doubtless had the dual effect of attributing a comprehensible cause to uncanny phenomena and reinforcing social taboos in eighteenth-century England. As criminals and suicides were those most commonly denied Christian burial, the implication was that such acts would result in a fate worse than mere physical death, as their souls would be refused access to Heaven and forced to wander the earth disconsolately until the Day of Judgement.

Belief that the spirits of suicides would walk after death was so ingrained in early modern society, that the corpses of individuals who had taken their own life were often pinned down in their graves and buried at crossroads to confuse their risen souls. An eighteenth-century Calderdale tradition held that following the suicide of Miller Lee of Mayroyd Mill in Hebden Bridge, his body was interred without ceremony at Four Lane Ends on the edge of Midgley Moor. However, his restless spirit proved such a menace to travellers passing by the crossroads, that his corpse was exhumed and reburied in a prehistoric cairn located on a more remote part of the moor, where his spectre could wander without causing disruption. Local folklore asserts that this Bronze-Age burial mound has been known as Miller's Grave ever since.

Miller's Grave in Calderdale, a prehistoric tumulus haunted by a suicide. (Kai Roberts)

The Busby Stoop near Thirsk, haunted by a gibbeted highwayman. (Kai Roberts)

The association between criminals and unhallowed burial did not have quite the same antiquity as suicides, and seems to be a very characteristic product of the eighteenth century. Although the use of gibbeting of a criminal's corpse after execution had been used informally since the previous century, it did not become common practice until it was officially authorised by an Act of Parliament in 1751, and remained widespread until it was outlawed in 1832. As the criminal's body was left to rot where it hung, in rural areas gibbets were often sited at crossroads to prevent their ghosts from walking and such traditions lingered long after the practice was discontinued. A pub known as the Busby Stoop, near Thirsk, was built on the former site of a gibbet, and it is still believed to be haunted by the restless spirit of Thomas Busby, a highwayman who was once gibbeted there. On bright moonlit nights, it is said that he can be seen leering from the window of the hostelry.

Of course, the innocent sometimes also suffered the ignominy of unconsecrated burial. Knaresborough vicarage was wracked by the sound of sobbing and icy gusts of wind through the corridors, until renovations uncovered human bones concealed beneath the floorboards. The remains were reinterred in consecrated ground and the trouble ceased. Likewise, a cottage at Barmby Moor occupied by two antiquaries was disturbed by untraceable footsteps and doors opening of their own accord – phenomena quickly attributed to a human skull the scholars had found in the churchyard. The relic had apparently been unearthed and cast aside by a gravedigger, so the pair had taken it for their private museum. Once reburied, the peace of their cottage was restored.

Battlefields also represented prime locations for spectral return. Not only were they the scenes of many tragic deaths, but often following the combat, the slain

Marston Moor, haunted by a victim of the Civil War conflict? (Kai Roberts)

were left to rot on the ground or else deposited in unconsecrated mass graves. The Battle of Marston Moor, fought between the Royalists and Parliamentarians on 2 July 1644 during the English Civil Wars, was one of the largest conflicts ever enacted on British soil, in which over 4,000 soldiers were killed. The site of the confrontation is also one of the first recorded instances of a battlefield ghost: a headless cavalry officer covered in blood, who is said to ride frantically back and forth, searching for the action. The apparition was most commonly seen around Moor Lane, where some of the fiercest fighting took place and where a monument to those killed now stands.

As these examples suggest, as the centuries wore on, ghosts went from primarily haunting people to haunting places. In medieval and early modern narratives, the exact location at which a ghost was encountered was rarely considered important and nor was it necessarily bound by it. However, by the eighteenth and nineteenth century, apparitions were nearly all fixed in space: whether it be the site of a terrible tragedy, unconsecrated burial or just one of those liminal points so often associated with the supernatural. As a feature of this development, the concept of the 'haunted house' grew increasingly prominent. Whilst ghosts may have appeared in buildings previously, they were typically a transient phenomena; the idea of the irredeemably haunted house, whose ghost disturbed generations of residents, was a later product and arguably one fostered by the emergence of Gothic literature in the late 1700s.

Interestingly, the ghosts that began to haunt houses in this period were more often felt or heard rather than seen, and whilst they were undoubtedly regarded as the spirit of some individual who had probably once lived there, they were not always identified with any specific person. Grassington Old Hall, for instance, was widely reckoned to be haunted and locals avoided passing that way at night, but the manifestations rarely amounted to much more than unearthly noises and the patter of disembodied feet on the staircase. Similarly, the peace at Easington Hall in Holderness (now demolished) was often shattered by rushing noises and the swish of a dress on the stairs, whilst a groaning, bellowing noise sometimes sounded from the cellar. Raydale House, near Semerwater, was particularly disturbed by a 'noisy spirit' known as 'Auld 'Opper', which used to rap on various items of furniture and knock furiously at the door.

Whilst these ghosts may have been raucous, they were never hostile and in the early nineteenth century at least, their nature seemed to be regarded as different from those violent manifestations which were regarded as the work of boggarts. However, it is difficult to tell how much this distinction was a product of the popular imagination at the time, and how much was imposed by the folklorists who recorded the material. Nonetheless, both seem to have been precursors to the modern 'poltergeist', which did not emerge as a separate category in the English tradition until 1848, when this German loanword was popularised by Catherine Crowe in her seminal compendium, *The Night Side of Nature*. Prior to this, such hauntings had been associated with demons and witchcraft as much as the spirits of the dead. Indeed, the connection has always been tenuous and poltergeists increasingly became regarded as psychic phenomena, rather than interventions from beyond the grave.

Yet, although the ghosts of the eighteenth and nineteenth centuries rarely seemed to be able to interact with the material world in the manner of a poltergeist, these restless spirits were often regarded as such a nuisance that they had to be laid. A dissolute former resident of Low Hall at Appletreewick, by the name of Thomas Preston, tormented the household with a variety of auditory phenomena: 'Unearthly sounds were often heard; the oaken rack rattled most mysteriously, doors banged fearsomely, the rafters often creaking with no apparent cause. On stormy nights hollowed sepulchral groans proceeded from the roof.' The tenants grew so disturbed by these occurrences that they eventually had the spirit confined to a spring in Dibb Gill, known thereafter as Preston's Well.

The motif of trapping troublesome ghosts in watery places was a common one, and the Blue Lady that haunted Heath Old Hall, near Wakefield, befell a similar fate. She was thought to be the ghost of Lady Bolles, a former owner of the hall who had died in 1662, leaving instruction that her bedchamber be shut up for evermore. When this command was violated some decades later, her apparitions began to be seen gliding through the passages of the house and the coach road leading up to it. Eventually, however, her spirit was condemned to a pool on the banks of the river to which she gave her name. Yet such exorcism rarely proved successfully; the Blue Lady was still occasionally seen at Heath Old Hall, much as the ghost of Sir Walter was seen at Calverley Hall some time after he was laid for 'as long as green holly grows'.

The failures of these exorcisms doubtless reflected the on-going anxiety which post-Reformation theology had fostered in the population regarding the supernatural. People did not have faith in the capacity of Protestant ministers to banish evil spirits and Reverend J.C. Atkinson records an occasion when an elderly Danby parishioner asked him to expel a spectre haunting her house: 'I told her at last I could not, did not profess to "lay spirits"; and her reply was "Ay, but if I had sent for a priest o' t' au'd church, he was a' deean it. They wur a vast mair powerful conjurers than you Church-priests".' This experience reaffirms just how much the ghost tradition in Yorkshire was a product of the Reformation and the theological debates that followed. Rather than rid the world of superstition, Protestantism had imbued the supernatural with a newly devilish intent, and found itself with no defence against ghosts or those who believed in them.

TEN

WATER LORE

English folklore brims with legends pertaining to water sources; from lakes and rivers to wells and springs. It is hardly surprising that the medium should have exerted such a powerful fascination over the superstitious mind. Water is a fickle, dualistic element: on the one hand, it is essential for the maintenance of life; but on the other, it can snatch life away in an instant. It has the capacity to both reflect or distort an image; to reveal or deceive, like an illusionist playing games. Meanwhile, water has strongly liminal connotations. On the purely corporeal plane, a watercourse can divide physical territories, representing a no-man's land between this bank and the yonder shore. We have seen how such thresholds resonated in the pre-modern psyche, and water embodies more than one boundary: it springs mysteriously forth from the hidden places of the earth and conceals a murky netherworld beneath its surface, forming a portal between this realm and another.

As many residents will attest, Yorkshire can be a very wet part of the country and whilst it does not have many natural lakes, it has no shortage of rivers and streams. A number of these can be quite treacherous – especially when they are in spate or must be crossed by means other than a bridge – so it seems natural that their danger should have been personified in an array of sinister genius loci. It is an impulse which has endured into modern times, and the successful 1973 public information film featuring the Spirit of Dark and Lonely Water is arguably a late twentieth-century expression of exactly the same imaginative process that once populated our lakes, rivers, ponds and bogs with kelpies, grindylows and all manner of comparable terrors.

The kelpie, or water-horse, is the most widespread image associated with water sources and whilst it is particularly characteristic of Ireland, Scotland and Wales,

The River Ure in spate in Wensleydale. (Kai Roberts)

northern England has its fair share as well. For instance, a stretch of the River Ure, near Middleham in Wensleydale, is believed to be plagued by just such a fiend, which 'riseth from the stream at eventide and rampeth along the meadows eager for prey.' It is thought to take at least one human victim per year and sometimes many more. Clearly in previous centuries the vicinity of Middleham was once an important crossing point over the River Ure, and the ford particularly hazardous after heavy rainfall, as similar remarks are made about its nature in the legend concerning the construction of Kilgram Bridge (*See* Chapter Six).

An even more famous water-horse haunts the Bolton Strid in Wharfedale. Of course, this notorious spot is an exemplary location for such a legend as it is universally regarded as one of the most dangerous stretches of water in the entire British Isles. At this point, the River Wharfe rapidly narrows from approximately 80 feet wide to a mere 8 feet over a distance of only 300 yards. The majority of the water has eroded downwards through the rock, meaning that the depth of the Strid is considerable and due to the ferocity of the current flowing through it, impossible to fathom accurately. The rocks surrounding the channel are often extremely slippery and over the ages, numerous foolhardy individuals have attempted to jump across the narrow breach; no one who has fallen into the Strid has ever survived and even their corpses go unrecovered.

One apocryphal legend holds that nearby Bolton Abbey was founded in the twelfth century on land donated to the Augustinian canons by Lady Alice de Romilly, after her son drowned in the Strid when his horse unsuccessfully tried to jump it during a hunt. The episode was immortalised by William Wordsworth in

The perilous Bolton Strid, where a fairy steed rides on May Day morn. (Kai Roberts)

his poem of 1807, 'The Force of Prayer', although sadly the legend does not appear to have any historical foundation. Another legend connected with the Strid holds that three sisters – the heiresses of Beamsley Hall – kept watch at the Strid one May Day morning, hoping to see its fearsome water-horse and that by expressing their dearest wishes to it, they might, by magic, be brought to fruition. However, these siblings ought to have known better; for the spectral steed is only seen to emerge from the churning white waters prior to a fatality and whilst they may have witnessed it ride, not one of the three sisters returned to Beamsley Hall that day.

Whilst horses seem to be the most common embodiment of a perilous river, more anthropomorphic spectres have also been recorded, and a ford across the River Dove in Farndale on the North York Moors was once renowned as the haunt of a spirit known as Sarkless Kitty. She was said to manifest in the form of a striking young maiden without a shred of clothing to preserve her modesty – hence the title 'Sarkless' which in the local dialect means 'without a dress'. Kitty was supposed to appear to young men on the opposite bank of the Dove and using her beauty, tempt them to their deaths in the treacherous waters. The ghost was associated with a Gillamoor girl called Kitty Garthwaite, who, in 1787, had committed suicide in the river after being abandoned by her fiancé and like so many suicides in that era, was refused burial in consecrated ground.

Yet, it seems that this connection is mistaken, for there is evidence to suggest that the spot was already regarded as haunted years before Kitty Garthwaite's death. It seems more likely that her story was attached to a much older water spirit, whose legend arose as an animistic personification of the River Dove. Either way, at the peak of local belief in the tale, from the late eighteenth to early nineteenth century, at least eighteen victims were attributed to Kitty. Following the death of a popular young farmer in 1809, local feeling ran so high that the vicar of Lastingham was summoned to perform an exorcism on the ford. It seems unlikely that any fewer people died in those dangerous waters as a result of such an intervention, but nonetheless, the country folk were satisfied that Kitty had been laid and refused to even mention her name thereafter, lest she rise to torment them again.

Although Yorkshire in not abundant is natural lakes, there are a few examples and, perhaps inevitably, their origins have been thoroughly mythologised by generations of country folk. Yet, the narratives which have accreted around them differ quite considerably from the motifs associated with rivers. For, whilst the latter display distinctly animistic – some might say 'pagan' – characteristics, Yorkshire's lake legends embody a firmly monotheistic milieu, communicating orthodox Christian theology regarding almsgiving and divine judgement. Like many traditions connected with the Devil (*See* Chapter Six), these stories seem to have arisen to provide local congregations with concrete examples of God's power, by taking a common migratory legend and relocating it to a setting familiar to the audience.

The most famous example concerns Semerwater, the largest natural lake in North Yorkshire and the second largest in the county as a whole. It nestles in the secluded confines of Raydale, a tributary valley of Wensleydale and is surely one of the most picturesque spots in that region. The legend tells that a prosperous settlement once stood where Semerwater lies today, and its wealth was such that the people of the town had grown proud and decadent. One day, an impoverished and elderly vagrant – some say a pious hermit – stumbled upon this community and went from door to door humbly asking for some provisions to help him on his way. But, such was the arrogance of the townsfolk, they refused to provide the old man with even a morsel of food and he was turned away from every house he visited.

At length, after he had been snubbed at every dwelling in the town, he came across a much less affluent residence high on the flanks of the surrounding valley. It was occupied by a poor shepherd and his wife, but despite their own hardship, they insisted the beggar partake in their meal and offered him shelter overnight. Thus, the following morning, before he travelled on, the old man looked down on the community that had treated him so poorly, raised his arms to the heavens and declaimed, 'Semerwater rise, Semerwater sink and swallow all the town, save yon li'l house where they gave me food and drink!' Sure enough, a deluge rose to consume the uncharitable town; but whilst it submerged the houses of all those who had turned the hermit away, the waters stopped just short of the cottage where he had found hospitality at last.

A similar tale is told of Gormire, a small body of water which lies beneath Whitestone Cliff on the edge of the Hambleton Hills. Gormire is an unusual lake in that no streams or rivers feed or drain it; rather it is a glacial feature sustained by a spring alone, but doubtless this curious composition helped foster the notion

Semerwater in Raydale, beneath which lies a sunken town. (Kai Roberts)

that it was bottomless. Local legend claims that it too was once the site of a wealthy town which was inundated following a terrible earthquake; however, the story is less clear on the connection between the pride of its inhabitants and its watery fate. Nonetheless, it was long believed that ruined buildings lay beneath the surface of Gormire and could be seen glinting in the depths when the waters were especially clear.

The sunken city is a common motif across the world and has been throughout the ages. As early as the fourth century BC, the Ancient Greek philosopher, Plato, implied that the legendary city of Atlantis was drowned by the gods as punishment for its leaders' hubris, and the trope also appears extensively in Celtic mythology – most pointedly in the Breton legend of Ys. Perhaps more significantly, the theme has parallels with the Judaeo-Christian tradition of the Great Flood, which the Book of Genesis claims God sent to express his displeasure with the sinfulness of mankind. The lesson of the deity's retribution against communities who prodigiously sinned or failed to exhibit virtues such as charity, was doubtless one that clergy, both Catholic and Protestant, wished to instil in their flock and by attaching this moral to a local landmark, sought to bring it closer to home.

Whilst Yorkshire may not have many natural lakes, it is rather more abundant in springs; especially those which have been dedicated to some patron saint and dubbed 'holy wells'. Indeed, according to one reckoning, the county has the highest density of such wells in England outside Cornwall, a region widely considered to be the home of the holy well. The precise definition of a 'holy well' is contested: some authorities use the title to refer solely to those wells which have been consecrated by the Christian Church, whilst other sources employ the term rather more loosely, applying it to any well that possesses some historic or cultural significance. In the interests of avoiding confusion, this chapter will go on to discuss the latter category, but it will reserve the title 'holy well' for the former alone.

There is also much controversy surrounding the provenance of well worship. For many generations it was popular to assume that holy wells were a direct survival from the animistic pre-Christian religions of the British Isles, and that a continuous tradition of veneration from that period could be identified at a number of examples. There are certainly understandable grounds on which to believe this: there is extensive evidence of votive offerings being deposited in water sources during the Iron Age and Romano-British period, and superficially, the medieval holy well tradition has much in common with such ancient practice. On the other hand, the rationale of the assumption depended greatly on the early folkloric hypothesis of 'survivals', which has long been discredited – at least as far as pagan survivals are concerned.

There are two substantial obstacles to supposing any demonstrable continuity of tradition in well worship from the pre-Christian period. Firstly, between the Romano-British period and the early Middle Ages, the Dark Ages intervenes. During this time, no written records exist to document the status of such belief through those centuries, and the archaeological record remains conspicuously silent on the matter. Secondly, the historical record suggests the pattern of use and abandonment of holy wells is so dynamic – even within the Middle Ages, let alone after the Reformation – that it would be quite remarkable if a tradition had endured for such a lengthy period of time. Therefore, it is more realistic to suggest that whilst Iron-Age Celts and medieval Christians may both have worshipped at wells, they probably worshipped at *different* wells. Very little evidence of the former survives and the latter took place firmly within the context of orthodox Christianity.

In his study of holy wells, folklorist Jeremy Harte suggests that those springs known simply as 'Holywell' may represent the earliest examples of sacred springs in the Christian tradition, in many cases pre-dating the Norman Conquest. He bases this conclusion on the extent to which these names are embedded in the landscape, in toponyms or family names such as Halliwell. Harte goes on to suggest that the distribution pattern of such wells – concentrated primarily in areas which would have been classed as 'waste' in the Domesday Book, but not too far from the periphery of civilisation – indicates that they were probably originally associated with hermits, and other mendicant holy men, in the period before many permanent churches were established. It is perhaps consistent then that springs baldly titled 'Holywell' are amongst the most ubiquitous in Yorkshire, especially the West Riding – for example, Halliwell Syke or Holywell Green, both in the vicinity of Halifax.

The second wave seems to have been those wells dedicated to native saints, of which there is an abundance in Yorkshire. It is with these early dedications that the reputation of holy wells for healing first emerged. According to Catholic doctrine, the souls of saints passed immediately into the presence of God and so could function as intercessors, who would communicate a supplicant's prayer to the Almighty. However, for the prayer to be more effective, it is desirable to be in close proximity to the saint's remaining traces on earth. It was through such belief that the medieval cult of relics flourished, to the point where almost every cathedral and monastery in the Middle Ages preserved bones, which they claimed were those of some beatified patron.

Hordes of pilgrims flocked to offer prayers to saintly relics and such was the demand for this service, that people began to consider that it was not just the mortal remains of saints that were efficacious; maybe the

St John's Well at Harpham, where St John of Beverley performed miracles. (Kai Roberts)

places and objects they had consecrated during their lifetime were similarly potent? As such, wells from which they had drunk and supposedly blessed came to act as substitute relics. It is true that such practices were regarded with contempt by some ecclesiastics, but their objections were not so much due to fear of paganism; rather, they were disturbed that they could not control and profit from the worship taking place at these sites. Their objections were about authority rather than theology. Conversely, there is evidence to suggest other churchmen not only tolerated well worship, but actually approved it.

However, much as saints' bones were easily faked, so were their wells. The only examples in Yorkshire which have a strong historical connection with their patrons are those dedicated to St Cedd and St Chadd at Lastingham, the former location of a monastery founded by those two clerics in the seventh century. However, whilst a number of wells around Whitby are dedicated to St Hilda, who established the abbey in the town during the same period, the traditions are so vague as to leave considerable room for doubt. Lady Hilda is supposed to have had a retreat near the wells dedicated to her at Hindwell and Aislaby, and often supped from Abbey Well at Hawsker, but there is no evidence to corroborate any of these traditions. It is also instructive that Christianity almost entirely died out around Whitby between the Viking invasion of AD 867 and its Norman restoration in 1078, and it is doubtful the name of her well could have survived two centuries of pagan Danish occupation.

Other notable examples of wells dedicated to indigenous saints in Yorkshire are equally suspect. St John's Well at Harpham is dedicated to St John of Beverley and the village claims to be the birthplace of the saint; unfortunately, contemporary sources make no reference to this fact and the tradition is not recorded before the sixteenth century. The long-lost St Robert's Well at Knaresborough rose on land close to St Robert's Cave, where the twelfth-century hermit is reputed to have lived, but there is evidence to suggest that it was an earlier Holywell rededicated to the local saint. Meanwhile, despite his well's popularity in the Middle Ages, there is no evidence to suggest that St Mungo ever visited Copgove; nor, for that matter, that St Augustine once preached beside St Austin's Well at Drewton and baptised new converts in its waters.

As the Middle Ages wore on, wells were increasingly dedicated to universal saints. In some cases, the dedication may have taken place as the result of a vision of the saint enjoyed by some rustic at that spot, much as shrines continue to spring up across the Roman Catholic world today. In other instances, the dedication may imply not that the well was considered sacred in itself, but simply that it provided the water supply for a nearby chapel. Lady Wells – dedicated to Our Lady, the Blessed Virgin Mary – were particularly common during this period, as the mother of Christ was considered to be a universal intercessor and proximity to her mortal traces was not necessary for prayers to her to be effective. In Yorkshire, examples are recorded at Hartshead, Brayton, Roche Abbey, Catwick and Threshfield to name but a few.

Wells dedicated to St Helen were also common in the late Middle Ages, especially in Yorkshire, with a famous example surviving at Eshton, near Gargrave, which is still venerated today. Indeed, some commentators have regarded St Helen as disproportionately attached to wells – her name is the most common dedication for holy wells but only twentieth for church dedications – and used this fact to suggest that this is a corrupt remembrance of the well's previous connection with some pre-Christian female water deity. However, St Helen may have had stronger links with Yorkshire than any pagan goddess. She was the mother of the Roman emperor, Constantine the Great, who Christianised the Roman Empire under her influence. As Constantine's father died in York, and it was from that city his own succession to emperor was proclaimed, a local medieval tradition held that Helen was a native of the area and this may have much to do with her association with holy wells in the county.

The Reformation attempted to sweep away well worship, like so many popular medieval Christian customs, once and for all. But, as in numerous other cases, it was only partially successful and whilst such veneration declined in the fifty years immediately following the dissolution of the monasteries, the continental fashion for spa waters ensured that it soon made a comeback, albeit in modified form. Although Protestantism found the doctrine of saintly intercession unconscionably idolatrous, it was not averse to the idea that 'heavenly grace was concentrated at particular locations'. However, they revised the mechanisms by which this was thought to occur, providing a pseudo-scientific veneer so that wells were thereafter venerated for their supposed miraculous mineral properties. Nonetheless, this led to the rejection of the pure water of many medieval holy wells, in favour of those with a high iron or sulphur content – and a correspondingly astringent flavour.

It was also during this period that certain holy wells developed a reputation for curing specific ailments. During the Middle Ages, saintly intercession was regarded as effective for any complaints but, now couched in medical terminology, the claims made for wells needed to be smaller and more credible. The most common disorders treated at wells from the sixteenth century onwards were connected with the eye: St Akelda's Well at Middleham, St Helen's Well at Eshton, St John's Well at Harpham and Lady Well at Threshfield were all known for their potency in this regard. Some other wells were more specialised: St Peter's Well at Barmby-on-the-Marsh was thought to treat scurvy; St Mungo's Well at Copgrove cured rickets; and St John's Well at Harpham was also known to tame wild animals. The only genuinely effective wells, however, were those whose unusually cold waters offered respite to rheumatics, such as St Peter's Well in Leeds.

Despite the scientific façade with which many wells were now presented, the rituals performed at them were still very much a product of the pre-modern mind. For instance, rather than take a course of the mineral water, a single draught or one-off bodily immersion was usually held to be sufficient for the well to work its cure. Meanwhile, one of the most widespread customs was for a visitor to tear a strip from their clothing and tie it to some branch beside the well; leaving it there symbolised leaving their infirmity behind and it was thought that as the rag decayed, so would their illness diminish. During the eighteenth and nineteenth century, it was often noted that the trees around the St Helen's Wells at Walton and Eshton were festooned with rags for this purpose. The practice was also noted at St Oswald's Well in Great Ayton, but the garment of the sick person was first thrown into the well; if it floated, then its owner would recover, but if it sank, the prognosis was dire.

Such divination was often frequently practiced at wells up until the nineteenth century. At St John's Well, near Mount Grace Priory, people wanting to make a wish would stick a pin through an ivy leaf and float it on the water; the direction in which the pin turned would indicate the likelihood of favourable response. More typically, lovesick girls would simply cast a crooked pin into the well whilst wishing for a vision of their future husband and this practice is extensively recorded at Lady Well in Brayton. The pins were believed to be an offering to the fairy who presided over the well, and a story from Brayton relates that the fairies wished to use the pins for their arrowheads, but having no power over iron they could only obtain it through such a trade. An association between fairies and wells was quite common in the eighteenth and nineteenth century, and it may be that the presiding fairy represented a corrupted memory of the well's former saintly patron.

However, the precise symbolism of the crooked pin is uncertain. Some writers have suggested a link to the ritually damaged votive offerings deposited by many prehistoric cultures, but like other connections between well worship and pre-Christian religions, this is tenuous at best. Oblations are a feature of many faiths and it is common to find offerings left at Christian shrines today. Hence, during the Middle Ages, the pin may have been connected to some more ornate item of jewellery and represented a more significant sacrifice, which eventually lost its meaning and value when mass-production of pins began during the Industrial Revolution. Meanwhile, crooked items were often considered 'lucky' in previous centuries, such as a crooked sixpence carried as a talisman and immortalised in the nursery rhyme.

It is clear that as the centuries passed and medical science advanced, the practice of praying for healing at wells had evolved into more generalised wishing. Whilst the rags that were tied to the trees around St Helen's Well at Walton may once have been intended to represent a visitor's ailment, the comments of nineteenth-century writers suggest they were now more typically left as an offering to ensure the fulfilment of their heart's desire. Sometimes there was a more elaborate ritual to be performed. For instance, anybody hoping for their wish to be granted at Lady Well, near Roche Abbey, had to take a sip of water from the well then hold it in their mouth whilst they walked backwards up the hillside and passed through a hole in an old tree, mentally repeating their wish the whole time.

Much as Protestantism had been unable to suppress the practice of leaving offerings at wells, it was similarly unable to defeat the popular notion that well waters were more potent on certain days of the year. In the case of holy wells with medieval provenances, this was still often the day of the feast of the saint to whom the well had been dedicated; whilst for post-Reformation spa wells, a more

Spaw Sunday celebrated in Cragg Vale. (John Billingsley)

universal holy day was chosen, such as Palm Sunday or Ascension Day. Lady Anne's Well near the ruins of Howley Hall at Morley in West Yorkshire was supposed to run with a variety of colours at six o'clock in the morning of Palm Sunday. Local legend added that sometime in the seventeenth century, a lady of Howley Hall by the name of Anne Saville, used to bathe in the well. On one such occasion, she fell asleep by its side, whereupon she was fatally attacked by some wild animals from the surrounding woods and the well was named in her memory.

The mill-workers of Batley and Birstall visited the well on Palm Sunday to take the chalybeate waters at St Anne's Well, and the annual Feldkirk Fair grew up around it. Such occasions would regularly see large crowds congregate at certain wells to drink the water and were the scene of much 'rowdyism'. In Calderdale, spa celebrations were held on the first Sunday in May, known as 'Spaw Sunday', and taken very seriously indeed. During the eighteenth and nineteenth centuries, great numbers of people from across the valley made pilgrimages to spa wells in Luddenden and Cragg Vale. The practice has recently been revived at the latter and now pilgrims process to the well from the church of St John in the Wilderness, although many are reluctant to taste the strongly sulphurous waters and content themselves with a sniff.

Of course, a well did not have to be known for its healing properties for a folk tradition to develop around it. The Ebbing and Flowing Well, near Giggleswick, is a particularly famous example whose waters can rise and fall by several inches,

The Ebbing and Flowing Well at Giggleswick — a transformed nymph? (Kathryn Wilson)

sometimes a number of times over the course of an hour. The action is caused by a complex geological siphon in the surrounding hillside, but in his epic topographical poem of 1612, 'Poly-Olbion', Michael Drayton records a more colourful tradition. He claims the area was once home to a beautiful but shy nymph, who had the misfortune to be seen by a lustful satyr. This beast pursued her with dark intentions and as his quarry grew weary from the chase, she fell down panting and begged the gods for salvation. In response, they took the curious decision to transform her into a spring:

> Even as the fearful nymph then thick and short did blow
> Now made by them a spring, so doth she ebb and flow.

Despite the fame of this legend, it is unlikely that it was a genuine local tradition and may be Drayton's invention entirely. Spirits such as nymphs and satyrs belong to Greco-Roman mythology, not Yorkshire folklore, and the tale seems more likely to have sprung from the imagination of an Oxford Classicist than a Craven hill-farmer. A more typically indigenous tale connected to the Ebbing and Flowing Well suggests it was once the retreat of an old wise-woman who gave the highwayman, Will Nevison, a magic bit for his mare; an artefact which allowed the horse to vault previously unimagined distances and so throw off pursuit. A number of limestone gullies in the Dales bear the title 'Nevison's Leap' and on one occasion, the horse is even reputed to have cleared the vast chasm of Gordale Scar.

Meanwhile, at Harpham, the beat of a drum was once supposed to echo from a well close to the old manor house upon the death of any member of the Quintin family, formerly squires of the village. It is said to be the spirit of Tom Hewson, who served as a drummer-boy to the Quintin family in the Middle Ages. Legend relates that he was knocked into the well during an archery tournament as an enraged Squire Quintin pushed past him to scold an incompetent contestant. By the time Tom's body was retrieved, he had drowned, much to the anguish of his mother, Molly Hewson, a local witch. In her grief, she decreed: 'Squire Quintin, you were the friend of my boy, but from your hand his death has come. Therefore, whenever a Quintin, Lord of Harpham, dies, my poor boy shall beat his drum at the bottom of this fatal well.' The site is known today as the Drumming Well and another such well was once recorded at nearby North Frodingham, but its tradition is less defined.

Phantoms are often associated with holy wells, but their legends are typically much more vague. A white lady wandered near Lady Well at Catwick, accompanied by the cry of an unseen baby; whilst a one-eyed, hooded woman haunted Holywell at Atwick, variously reputed to be the spirit of a murder victim buried there, or a nun from nearby Nunkeeling Priory. Equally, many wells – such as Thruskell Well near Burnsall – were regarded as the haunt of generic entities such as Jenny Greenteeth or Peg-o-the-Well, who would drag children who got too close into the well's murky depths. Doubtless such stories were widely employed by

The Drumming Well at Harpham from which a drum beats on the death of a local noble. (Kai Roberts)

Lady Well at Threshfield, whose waters could ward off evil spirits. (Kai Roberts)

cautious parents trying to keep their children from drowning, but often the role of 'bogeyman' was the final function of a belief that had once been sincerely held by the adult community (*See* Chapter Eight).

However, wells were not universally favoured by spirits: in some instances, their consecrated waters were an effective defence against them and such was the case at Lady Well, near Threshfield. Local legend reports that Threshfield Grammar School was once sorely troubled by a ghost known as Pam the Fiddler, who resembled a 'wizened owd man, summat of a monkey sort, covered with soft downy hair.' Old Pam was a merry spirit who was often heard to fiddle all night in the schoolrooms, accompanied by the shouts and laughter of his spectral party guests, whilst an uncanny illumination streamed from the windows. Many locals were quite fond of Pam, but the schoolmasters hated him and frequently complained about his presence distracting the pupils, as he paced the upper floor or slammed doors shut with abandon.

One night, a drunken tinker named Daniel Cooper was passing by the school at a late hour as he returned home from the pub. Seeing that eerie light from the windows, he knew that Pam's revels must be in full swing and thought to spy on their carousing. Unfortunately, however, he attracted the attention of the assembled spirits with a sneeze, and, furious with the tinker's imposition, they pursued him into the night. Fearful for his soul, Daniel took refuge in the middle of nearby Lady Well, but whilst Pam and his entourage dare not pluck their prey from its sacred waters, they remained on guard at a safe distance. As a result, Daniel was forced to spend the night immersed up to his neck in bitterly cold water, until the cock finally crowed and dawn drove the ghosts away. Yet, despite his ordeal in the icy well, he is said to have emerged with renewed vigour – doubtless a testament to the healing properties of those holy waters.

ELEVEN

SECRET TUNNELS AND BURIED TREASURE

Secret tunnels are one of the most ubiquitous motifs in English folklore: in every locality, there is bound to be some tavern, church, mansion or ruin to which the legend of a hidden conduit is attached. In many cases, these rumours of lost subterranean passages have survived into the present day, whilst they have been reinvented for recent generations through tales of Cold War nuclear bunkers and classified government installations. These mysterious underground networks seem to exert a powerful influence over the collective psyche and no matter how many times the reports are debunked, belief in their existence persists.

There are good reasons for this. Over the centuries, actual secret tunnels have been constructed – then forgotten about and rediscovered – for numerous purposes: for instance, to enable smugglers to evade the Customs & Excise men; to permit nobles to escape a besieged castle; or to allow priests access to a Catholic house unhindered during the Reformation. Equally, old buildings often seem to display signs of such clandestine passageways, although when properly excavated they mostly prove to be little more than the remains of an ancient drain or ice-house.

Pseudo-historical narrative and superficial evidence are woven around every tunnel rumour to lend a veneer of plausibility, which can whet the appetite of even the most circumspect local historian. Typically, however, the game is often given away by the impossibility of the structure. The tunnels of local folklore invariably run an unfeasible length or traverse impractical terrain. Some are supposed to pass beneath rivers, where the workings would quickly flood and collapse, or between points of radically different altitude. Whilst our ancestors were often remarkable engineers, such feats were undoubtedly beyond them.

As if secret tunnels were not themselves sufficiently stimulating to the imagination, they also proved fertile ground for more fantastic speculation. Supernatural entities frequently haunted these passages, from beasts guarding them from unwelcome incursions to ghosts tracing the route as they had done in life. Following his leap from Scar Top at Netherton, the Devil still wanders the network of tunnels beneath Castle Hill near Huddersfield, whilst only a short distance away at Lepton, the headless ghost of Sir Richard 'Black Dick' Beaumont stalks the course of a tunnel between Whitley Hall and a folly known as Black Dick's Tower.

Tunnels are also known as one of many repositories for that other staple of local legend – buried treasure. Again, such rumours have a greater credibility than many pre-modern folk beliefs. Prehistoric and Anglo-Saxon burial mounds have been known to yield valuable grave goods, whilst prior to the existence of a proper banking system, burial was often the only way of securing personal wealth against the vicissitudes of fortune. During troubled times from the Roman occupation through the Dark Ages to the medieval period, men of property have entrusted their savings to the earth and for various reasons, never returned to reclaim it.

Archaeologist-cum-folklorist Leslie Grinsell, who made a study of treasure legends relating to prehistoric sites, remarked, 'It is natural that in regions where explorations resulted in finding objects of material value, folk traditions of buried treasure would develop and not only become attached to sites where treasure may have been found, but also spread to other barrows in the region and ancient monuments generally.' Indeed, across Yorkshire legends of buried treasure are found associated not only with prehistoric burial mounds, but standing stones, waymarkers and the ruins of castle or monasteries.

It is not difficult to see the appeal of legends concerning buried treasure. The prospect of acquiring wealth, without any of the attendant labour so often involved, is attractive in any age. However, it is clear that during the medieval and early modern period, such legends were taken very seriously indeed. By 1542, so many wayside crosses and boundary markers were being pulled down in the belief that riches lay buried below, that Henry VIII was moved to enact a statute proscribing treasure-hunting. Meanwhile, local gossip often attributed the financial ascendance of certain families to the discovery of buried treasure, and 'hill-digger' was a popular term of abuse for the nouveau-riche of the age.

Like secret tunnels, some treasure legends came with a suggestion of historical authenticity. The Nortons of Craven were a wealthy local family in the Middle Ages believed to have hidden their fortune in Norton Tower, their hunting lodge on Rylstone Fell, prior to the family's extinction following their support for the Pilgrimage of Grace. Similarly, during the 1745 rising, a Jacobite hoard had supposedly been buried in a curious knoll known as Silver Hill at Stanbury, a region of the county in which many members of the local gentry had been sympathetic to the Young Pretender's doomed claim to the British throne. As late as 1899, local author Halliwell Sutcliffe noted, 'The fields which climb this hill were well tilled aforetime through being constantly turned over in search of the treasure.'

Yet, whilst some such legends exhibit a semblance of probability, there is a far greater corpus which seem overtly incredible. Not only are these treasures located in impossible topographies, revealed or guarded by strange supernatural beings, the associated narratives also employ a body of phantasmagorical symbolism, the key to which we have long since forgotten. As a result, some of these stories appear quite impenetrable today, albeit in a pleasingly dreamlike fashion. Yet, it undoubtedly seems as if the legends are meant to encode some esoteric knowledge or some valuable moral, offering much opportunity for febrile speculation.

The ruins of Gisborough Priory, location of buried treasure. (Kai Roberts)

Certainly, in many narratives, the unobtainable nature of the treasure is emphasised. An archetypal version of these legends is attached to Gisborough in Cleveland, where a tunnel was rumoured to run over a mile from the ruined priory to a district known as Tocketts. At the midway point of this tunnel, there was supposedly a large chest of gold constantly watched over by a bird of the corvid family. When one brave individual attempted to procure the treasure for himself, he found himself 'terribly used by its guardian, the crow, which suddenly became transformed into His Satanic Majesty.' In later folklore, a phantom black monk prowls the priory ruins to guard the treasure against seekers.

A variation on this tale is told about the prehistoric earthwork (possibly an Iron-Age enclosure) known as Maiden Castle, on Harkerside in Swaledale. Although the treasure buried beneath was notorious, legend maintained that only one band of fortune-hunters had ever actually laid eyes on it. When they tried to open the chest, a black hen appeared and flapped her wings so violently that it put out their light, and left them unable to approach the chest. This happened three times and eventually the men had to quit. They returned the following day, but this time they were assailed by such a ferocious storm that they never even found the chest again.

Birds of some description – typically corvids or poultry – are frequently portrayed as the guardians of the treasure, although in some instances they are accompanied by other incongruous beasts. Indeed, these more elaborate narratives tend to be bizarre in several respects. For instance, a legend attached to the ruins of Kirkstall Abbey, near Leeds, tells the story of a local man who had a particularly curious experience involving a hidden tunnel, mysterious treasure and its unusual guardians.

Maiden Castle, a prehistoric enclosure above Swaledale and the location of buried treasure. (Kai Roberts)

Kirkstall Abbey near Leeds, location of buried treasure. (Kai Roberts)

This Kirkstall man had been threshing corn in the abbey grounds and as he was taking a break at midday, he observed a cavity in the ruins which he had never noticed before. Further investigation revealed an underground passage which, in the spirit of inquiry, he pursued for some considerable distance until it suddenly opened out, and he discovered himself standing in a great hall with a fire blazing in the hearth. Even more oddly, a black horse stood in one corner, behind which sat a large oaken chest with a cock watching over it.

Suspecting the chest contained treasure, the man resolved to acquire it for himself and approached. However, as he drew closer 't'horse whinnied higher and higher, and cock crowed louder and louder, an when he laid his hand on t'kist, t'horse made such a din, an t'cock crowed and flapped his wings, and summat fetched him such a flap on t'side of his head as felled him flat an he knowed nowt more till he came to hisself and he war lying on't common.' The man searched for the entrance to that secret passage many times over the years, but he was never able to find it again.

A similar, but even more surreal story is told about the ruined fourteenth-century hunting tower known as Dob Park Lodge in Washburndale. At the foot of the remains of the staircase, there is a debris-choked aperture which must once have led to the cellars, and this had long been a source of rumour and intrigue locally. One night, a notorious 'n'er-do-well' of the district, under the influence of alcohol, resolved to explore the tunnel and a crowd of neighbours gathered above to await his return. The brave man did not return for some considerable time, but just as his friends were starting to grow genuinely concerned, he suddenly erupted from the depths in a state of great terror.

When the man had collected himself, he explained that he had followed the passage a great distance until he began to grow weary. Yet at the very moment he had resolved to turn back, an unearthly music began to fill the air around him, and the sound so cheered him that it drew him on. He never discovered the source of that music, but eventually he stumbled into a vast room 'as big as any church', lit by another blazing fire in the hearth. In the centre of the room was a table with a glass set out, and against the wall a great chest bound with iron bands and three locks, above which hung a great broadsword.

Beside the hearth stood 'a great, black, rough dog, as big as any two or three mastiffs' and the explorer was taken aback when this creature proceeded to address him in a human voice. It said, 'Now, my man, as you've come here, you must do one of three things, or you'll never see daylight again. You must either drink all the liquor there is in that glass, open that chest or draw that sword.' Apparently unfazed by this miraculous speech, the man surveyed his options and concluded that the chest looked too well-secured to open, and the sword too heavy for him to lift, so he opted to drink from the glass.

However, when the fluid touched his lips he found that it scalded hotter than any boiling water and, as he swigged, an invisible hand drew the sword and the lid of the

Dob Park Lodge in Washburndale, location of buried treasure and a talking dog. (Kai Roberts)

chest sprang open, revealing it to be brimming with gold. Taken aback, he slammed the glass down, causing it to shatter, whereupon his lantern and the fire were instantly extinguished. The mysterious music also abruptly ceased, to be replaced by a frightful howling and yelling, whilst something right beside him began to scream. He fainted, and after coming round in the darkness, fled the tunnel as quickly as he possibly could.

Yet another story in this vein is told of Richmond Castle in North Yorkshire. On one of his regular perambulations around Castle Hill, local man Potter Thompson was surprised to see a cavern in the hillside that he had never noticed before. He summoned up his courage to pursue the tunnel and after stumbling through the debris-choked darkness for some time, he encountered a great boulder which seemed to have been deliberately placed to prevent further progress. However, Thompson was not deterred and succeeded in traversing the stone, whereupon he found himself in a large chamber, radiant with a supernatural light and glittering with crystals, spars and stalactites.

In the centre of the chamber, there was a rocky table upon which lay a figure wearing armour and a crown, whilst on the floor surrounding him, twelve knights were similarly prostrate. A great shield balanced next to the table and Thompson recognised the crest upon it as that of the legendary King Arthur. Clearly this was where he and his knights had been taken following the hero's death at the Battle of Camlann, to lie in an enchanted slumber until such a time as England needed them again – a conviction first mentioned by William of Malmesbury in his 1125 work, *Gesta Regum Anglorum*.

Richmond Castle, resting place of the legendary King Arthur? (Kai Roberts)

The awestruck Thompson also noticed that a horn and sheathed sword hung from a wall of the cavern, and unable to resist his curiosity, attempted to draw the sword from its scabbard. As he did so, he noticed that the knights began to stir from their timeless rest and terrified by this development, he immediately replaced the sword and fled. But, as Thompson ran, a disembodied voice resounded through the tunnel: 'Potter Potter Thompson! If thou had'st either drawn the sword or blown the horn, thoud'st be the luckiest man that ever yet was born!' Some time afterwards, when he had recovered his nerve, Thompson attempted to return to the cavern and claim whatever fortune he had turned away from. Of course, he could never locate the opening again.

Although this is one of the few Arthurian legends in Yorkshire (he is also supposed to sleep beneath Freeborough Hill near Guisborough), the form is a familiar one. The King in the Mountain or Sleeping Hero motif is found across Europe and is associated with numerous semi-legendary figures, such as Charlemagne and Frederick Barbarossa. In the British Isles, the story is also told of Owain Lawgoch, Fionn MacCumhaill and Thomas the Rhymer, whilst King Arthur himself is reputed to be sleeping beneath various other locations including Craig y Dinas in Snowdonia, Sewingshields Castle in Northumberland and Alderley Edge in Cheshire.

A second legend is also attached to Richmond Castle, which claims that some decades after Potter Thompson's adventure, a troop of soldiers garrisoned at the castle sent a drummer boy into a tunnel they found in the cellars, which

Freeborough Hill, resting place of the legendary King Arthur? (Kai Roberts)

supposedly led to Easby Abbey and was believed to contain treasure. He was to drum as he proceeded and the soldiers would trace his route on the surface by listening for the sound. They followed his progress for about a mile or so before the drum suddenly stopped. The soldiers assumed the roof of the passage had caved in on the boy and placed a stone on the surface to mark the point where he fell. It is said that at midnight on certain nights, a ghostly drum beat can be heard in the vicinity of this stone.

Whilst legendary treasure is often represented as unobtainable by virtue of its supernatural guardians, in some narratives there are also certain rituals which must be performed to obtain the hoard successfully, and which are invariably either impossible to complete or botched at the last minute. At Beauchief Abbey near Sheffield, treasure supposedly lies in a secret tunnel running to Norton Church. This chest is not only guarded by a cock which starts to crow as soon as anybody goes near, but as S.O. Addy notes: 'The box can only be fetched away by a white horse, who must have its feet shod the wrong way round and who must approach the box with his tail foremost. The box must be tied to the horses head and not fastened behind.'

At Middleham in Wensleydale, there are two mounds south of the castle known as Williams Hills – almost certainly the remains of a Norman motte-and-bailey. No detail is given of the nature of the treasure buried here, only that, 'Whoever shall run nine times round without stopping shall find a door open in the mound, which will admit him to marvellous treasures.' Circling nine times is a common stipulation to invoke spirits or gain access to the Otherworld – one writer characterises the practice as 'unscrewing the barrier between these dual existences' – and the association with old mounds here suggests that this was imagined as a fairy treasure.

Not far from Middleham, on the shapely hill of Addleborough, there is a prehistoric burial cairn, known as Stone Raise, beneath which a treasure is supposed to lie. Legend records that it was accidentally dropped here by a weary giant as he attempted to transport it from Skipton Castle to Pendragon Castle in the Vale of Eden. When it hit the ground, the casket sank into the earth and stones rose over it. Anybody seeking to recover the chest will encounter 'a fairy in the form of a hen or an ape', but they must proceed in absolute silence. If this condition is broken, the fairy will vanish along with the treasure.

Even if silence was not demanded, then in some narratives certain taboos such as cursing would undoubtedly cause a treasure-hunting enterprise to fail. The renowned fairy hill of Willy Howe, in East Yorkshire, was also supposed to contain treasure, beyond the silver cup stolen from the Still Folk by the passing farmer in William of Newburgh's tale. William Hone's *Table Book* records that a farmer once dug the Howe to uncover a large chest of gold, which he then attempted to dislodge using 'a train of horses, extending upwards of a quarter of a mile, attached to it by strong iron traces.' Just as it was nearly out, the farmer exclaimed, 'Hop Perry, prow Mark! Whether God's will or not, we'll have this ark!' This thoughtless blasphemy caused all the iron traces to snap and the chest to sink deeper into the hill, leaving it beyond the farmer's reach for evermore.

Often in these legends there is the implication that mere greed debars a person from happily obtaining the treasure, but that it will be delivered to those who are truly in need. Another tale recounts how an old woman of Sexhow appeared to a neighbouring farmer after her death, and instructed the man to dig beneath a certain tree in his orchard to uncover a buried hoard. The apparition told him that he could have the silver for himself, but he should turn the gold over to her niece who was very poor. The farmer did as he had been bidden, and sure enough found the treasure; but rather than provide for the old woman's niece, he elected to keep it all for himself.

As William Henderson writes, 'From that day, however, he never knew rest or happiness … Every night, at home or abroad, Nanny's ghost failed not to dog his steps and reproach him with his faithlessness.' The end came one evening when his neighbours witnessed the farmer returning from Stokesley market, his horse galloping so furiously that it never stopped for the gate, but bounded straight over it. As he passed, the farmer was heard to cry, 'I will, I will, I will!' and keen observers claimed that an old lady in a black dress and straw hat sat behind him on the horse. However, when the beast finally came to a halt, only one figure was found still on its back – the corpse of the avaricious farmer.

Ghosts were not the only nocturnal visitants to reveal the location of buried treasure; dreams often disclosed such secrets. A tumulus known as Picts' or Money Hill, near Pickhill in North Yorkshire, had long been rumoured to contain a great fortune. One of Mother Shipton's prophecies had foretold that the village would never thrive until a local family became extinct and Picts' Hill was cut open. Meanwhile, in the early nineteenth century, a villager had dreamt that beneath the hill stood an archway beneath which there was a black chest, secured with three locks (like that at Dob Park), containing the fabled hoard.

In 1850, the local family did indeed reach extinction as specified in the prophecy and the following year, the Leeds and Thirsk Railway Company were constructing a track in the Pickhill region. Although it was not a necessary part of the building work, the directors were so intrigued by the tale of the treasure that they resolved to open Picts' Hill, and even enlisted the now very old dreamer to show them where to dig. Sadly, nothing was found other than a few cremation urns and an iron band, which may once have crested a helmet. However, the whole episode is a fine illustration of how seriously even educated men treated such legends up until the nineteenth century.

A young servant girl in Thoresby was rather more fortunate in her visions. She claimed to have dreamt that a treasure was buried in a certain place around the farm on which she worked and, sure enough, when she dug there, she discovered 'a bronze vessel containing a great quantity of coins.' Unluckily, the local landowner heard of the find and laid claim to it, but as the girl had already given a majority away to friends and relatives, she was forced to flee the district. According to Edmund Bogg, writing in the late nineteenth century, there were still many around Thoresby who claimed to possess coins from the hoard.

A far more fanciful story is attached to Upsall Castle in the Hambleton Hills. An old man of the district is supposed to have dreamt three nights in a row that if he travelled to London Bridge 'he would hear something to his advantage'. He was so impressed by the persistence of the dream that he walked all the way to the capital, a distance of more than 200 miles, and proceeded to wait on the bridge for some considerable length of time. Just as he was beginning to think the journey had been a wild goose chase, a Quaker approached and asked him what he had been waiting so long for.

The old man told him of the dream, to which the Quaker replied that he too had been subject to a recurring dream, in which he was told that a great treasure was buried beneath a particular bush in Upsall Castle yard. However, as he did not know where Upsall was, he had been unable to act upon it. Craftily, the old man denied any knowledge of Upsall, but as soon as he returned to the village, he set about digging beneath bushes in the castle yard until his spade hit upon the treasure.

The hoard of gold proved to be contained in a pot which bore an inscription that nobody in the area could translate. Content with his new fortune, the old man showed little curiosity regarding its meaning and donated the vessel to the village inn, where it was placed on display. One day, a bearded Jewish stranger stopped at the hostelry and told the villagers that the inscription read,

Look lower – where this stood
Is another twice as good.

On further investigation, not only did the villagers discover a second, much larger hoard, but yet another one below that, double its value again!

Whilst many of the narratives of buried treasure related in this chapter are clearly migratory legends – found with minor local variations at numerous locations across the north of England – none are quite so widely spread as that associated with Upsall. Not only are similar stories told about Swaffham Church in Norfolk and Dundonald Castle in South Ayrshire, but the earliest recorded example is found in a poem by the thirteenth-century Persian poet, Rumi, and a prose version was included in the famed collection of Arabian folktales, *One Thousand and One Nights*. However, this is only true of the first part of the narrative; the coda pertaining to the inscription on the pot and the further two hoards seems to be unique to Upsall.

Where dreams were not available to reveal the whereabouts of hidden treasure, sorcerous assistance was frequently called upon. Grimoires from the sixteenth and seventeenth centuries often contain instructions for the creation of a divination device referred to as a 'Mosaical Rod' for the purposes of treasure-hunting. Indeed, the use of forbidden magic in pursuit of treasure was clearly such a common phenomenon that in his statute of 1542, Henry VIII specifically condemns 'Invocacons and conjuracons of Sprites, ptending by such meanes to understande and get Knowledge for their owne lucre in what place treasure of golde and Silver shulde or mought be founde or had in the earthe or other secrete places.'

In 1509-10, this connection between magic and treasure-hunting led to one of the most extraordinary episodes in the folklore and social history of Yorkshire, all recorded for posterity in the Archiepiscopal Registers of York. Nine men of various social backgrounds came together to seek a legendary treasure said to be buried on Soil Hill, between Halifax and Bingley. Not only does the whole affair once again vividly illustrate how seriously such legends were once taken by educated men, but how seriously the authorities treated the matter, especially where suggestions of witchcraft were involved.

The conspirators were a motley crew. The matter seems to have been raised by a twenty-eight-year-old servant, William Wilson, to his master, a Bingley yeoman named William Otewell and a local priest called John Wilkinson. They enlisted two further priests, Richard Greenwood of Heptonstall and James Richardson of York, along with Knaresborough cunning-man, John Stewart, for magical assistance. The party was completed by Thomas Jameson, a wealthy merchant who had previously served as both Sheriff and Lord Mayor of York, along with two commoners by the names of Thomas Wood and Laurence Knolles.

Wilson had described the treasure as 'a chest of gold … and every noble (coin) as thick as five and upon the same chest a sword of maintenance and a book covered with black leather.' However, the expedition was clearly perceived by those involved as a dangerous venture. Richard Greenwood's father, Edward, claimed to have known men who had seen the treasure but failed to acquire it. A man called Leventhorp had allegedly found the chest guarded by a demon, who snapped the adventurer's sword 'as it had been a rush'. Even a monk from Sawley Abbey had been unable to overcome it. Meanwhile, John Wilkinson had suggested the treasure could not be obtain without sacrificing a human soul.

To this end, considerable magical preparation was necessary. Cunning-man, John Stewart, had already been censured by the ecclesiastical courts for having 'used false and damnable conjurations, invocations and divinations', whilst despite being a priest, James Richardson was 'publicly notorious for heresy and divination'. The expedition was further equipped with sacramental wafers; an incense censer; a sceptre; two stoles; a holy-water sprinkler; several books; a magic circle made from virgin parchment; and a 'lamen' – a talisman of metal inscribed with magical formulae for the desired outcome.

In this case, the lamen was a square of lead with a name on each side and a crude figure in the centre labelled 'Oberon'. Oberon was commonly mentioned in fifteenth-century grimoires and was typically portrayed as a trustworthy spirit who would lend assistance to humans in return for due respect. The party also seems to have planned to summon the Enochian demon Belphares, who, according to one later source, was known for his harmless nature and ability to locate and carry treasure.

However, the expedition was plagued by misfortune and never reached the stage where such invocations were necessary. The party set out on Tuesday, 29 January 1510, leaving from different directions and at different times to prevent such a large and incongruous group raising suspicion in the neighbourhood. Richardson, Jameson, Stewart and Otewell set off from one side of Bingley; Wilkinson, Wilson and Knolles from another. Meanwhile, Greenwood and Wood were travelling from Heptonstall and had arranged to rendezvous with the others at a wayside cross at the west end of Soil Hill, in the township of Northowram.

The seven men from Bingley assembled first at a farm near Wilsden, before proceeding to Soil Hill. Although it was night, there was an almost full moon and the hill should have been easily visible to them. Yet at this point, a thick mist descended and the party lost their way so badly that they found themselves in the village of Clayton, some distance to the east, and then proceeded to stumble in Mickle Moss, a tract of peat bog to the west of Queensbury. Eventually, they found a cross but it turned out to be the wrong one. Wilkinson, Otewell and Knolles volunteered to form an advance party and return for the others, but despite encountering a local who they paid 2d to lead them to the correct cross, they failed once more.

As the folklorist John Billingsley notes of the party, 'If they had any superstitious feelings at all ... they must have felt that fate, or something else, was not on their side.' Consequently, hungry and exhausted after their many defeats, the party eventually abandoned the mission for that night and returned to Bingley. On the journey back, they resolved to gather the following day to summon Belphares in Harden Wood and hope he could lead them to the treasure from there.

However, the plans must have been hastily made for John Wilkinson failed to appear at the meeting and without his assistance the invocation could not proceed. The assembled men turned to discussing how they should split the treasure, despite not yet being in possession of it, and perhaps inevitably, acrimony arose. Thomas Jameson argued that as a gentleman, he should have the largest share. Wilson and others unsurprisingly disagreed, lobbying for the spoils to be divided equally, which angered Jameson to such an extent, that he threatened to report the whole venture to the authorities.

Whether Jameson went ahead with his threat, or whether word got out some other way, is not recorded, but on 5 May 1510, the Vicar-General of the Archbishop of York called him before the ecclesiastical court and over the following month, the other eight men were summoned to appear on charges of heresy and sorcery. Having been found guilty on 11 June, they were commanded to assemble outside York Minster the following Sunday, where they were whipped and ordered to process barefoot along a prescribed route, whilst carrying banners representing their crimes and stopping at certain points for further whipping. The punishment was repeated in Bingley some weeks later.

TWELVE
ROBIN HOOD

Whilst Robin Hood is irrevocably associated with Sherwood Forest in the popular consciousness, the earliest sources for the legend suggest that the outlaw was as much at home in Yorkshire as Nottinghamshire. These sources show that the activities of Robin and his men were centred around an area of South Yorkshire known as Barnsdale, and although they are shown ranging across much of northern England and the north Midlands, no other location is described with such topographic detail. The area is so integral to the original ballads that many scholars suspect the legend was born in Barnsdale, and only migrated outwards over subsequent centuries as travelling balladeers sought to add local colour to their material.

Some local historians – most notably Hallamshire antiquarian Reverend Joseph Hunter in the nineteenth century, and President of the Yorkshire Archaeological Society, J. W. Walker, in the twentieth – have even attempted to identify an historical model for the character in the region. Their favoured candidate is a fourteenth-century citizen of Wakefield by the name of Robert Hood; but whilst the hypothesis has attracted a great deal of support within the county, the argument is largely circumstantial and there is a body of contradictory evidence to weigh against it. Indeed, many historians studying the legend now argue that it may be impossible to uncover an 'historical Robin'. The available data from the period is simply too slender to construct a compelling case and many attempts succumb to what J.C. Holt refers to as 'pseudo-history expressing local patriotism'.

It may simply be that there is no historical model for the legend. 'Robin Hood' perhaps began as a generic term for an outlaw – much as 'Jack Straw' was used in the late medieval period to signify any political agitator – and this archetype was then fleshed out by the balladeers' imagination. Indeed, some have contended that a focus on the character's historical existence is overly reductive and misses the symbolic richness of the legend itself. The earliest narratives tell us much about the concerns of late medieval society in England, whilst their subsequent development reveals how those concerns have changed over the centuries and demonstrates the versatility of the legend, as it has adapted to express them.

As a book primarily concerned with county folklore, this chapter will not deal extensively with the historical debate. Rather, the focus will remain on the legendary narratives themselves and the extent to which they are related to the topography of Yorkshire. For not only do the early ballads establish Barnsdale as Robin's primary stomping ground, as the legend migrated, later works placed him in numerous other locations across the county and local folklore developed a variety of apocryphal connections, expressed through tall tales, popular idioms and countless toponyms. Whilst Nottinghamshire might be able to boast Sherwood Forest, it is doubtful that any other county can claim as many sites associated with Robin's name as Yorkshire.

The legend was well established by 1377, as a reference to the 'rhymes of Robin Hood' in William Langland's allegorical poem 'William's Vision of Piers Plowman' attests. But whilst there are a number of tantalising textual allusions over the next 100 years, it is not until the mid to late fifteenth century that any complete narratives survive. The bulk of this material takes the form of ballads; these had doubtless been widely sung throughout the late medieval period, but could only be recorded for posterity by the emerging technology of the printing press. A few fragments of plays also survive and it is possible that the stories were transmitted in such dramatic forms long before they formalised into ballads.

Anybody accustomed to the legend as it is told today is likely to be surprised by the content of the ballads. Popular characters such as Maid Marian and Friar Tuck are missing, whilst as much emphasis is placed on Little John and Will Scarlett as Robin himself. Furthermore, many familiar themes are conspicuous by their absence. There is no suggestion that Robin was a Saxon peasant fighting Norman oppressors; instead he is repeatedly described as a yeoman, and doubtless the legend's popularity was aided by the growing influence of that class during the late Middle Ages. Similarly, the pagan overtones imputed by Victorian folklorists and emphasised in some modern adaptations are negligible. Although Robin is opposed to the Church as an institution, he remains personally faithful, especially to the Virgin Mary.

Perhaps most noticeably, Robin's redistributive tendencies are barely hinted at in the early ballads. Although he is presented as an honest thief who only robs from the rich, there is little evidence of him giving to the poor. This aspect of the legend does not seem to have emerged until the seventeenth century. Nonetheless, the medieval sources still portray Robin as something of an anti-authoritarian figure, with the principle targets of their ire being corrupt institutions, including the Church and regional authorities such as the Sheriff of Nottingham. The persistence of the legend through the late Middle Ages suggests that there was widespread hostility towards such bodies during that period, and the ballads ably reflected such sentiments.

There is some dispute over the antiquity of many of the ballads. Whilst several can be securely dated to the late fifteenth century, their venerability is very much an artefact of preservation. It is possible that some ballads which do not survive in print before the seventeenth century, were actually contemporary with or predated the fifteenth-century examples. For instance, the earliest surviving manuscript of the ballad 'Robin Hood and Guy of Gisbourne' comes from the mid-seventeenth century, but its similarities to a fragment of a play dated to 1475 indicate that it had probably been in circulation since that period at least. Conversely, one of the most significant early ballads, 'A Gest of Robyn Hode' – the earliest printings of which date to the 1490s – shows evidence of having been compiled from shorter ballads, individual versions of which do not survive in print until much later.

The 'Gest' is distinctive amongst the early ballads in that it has an epic structure and appears to attempt to relate a complete 'life' of Robin Hood. Where most ballads simply narrate single episodes, the 'Gest' features a number of instalments concluding with the death of the hero. It is also one of the most notable sources to locate Robin's activities in Barnsdale. Whilst the early ballads 'Robin Hood and the Potter' (c. 1500) and 'Robin Hood & Guy of Gisbourne' both refer to the region, the 'Gest' includes a wealth of topographic description which corresponds exactly with the actual geography; and even though action is divided between Barnsdale and Sherwood, as J.C. Holt observes, 'The legendary Barnsdale is by far the most detailed … Barnsdale seems real. Sherwood is somewhat like "the wood near Athens" of *A Midsummer Night's Dream*.'

The area referred to as Barnsdale is roughly defined and the title largely redundant today. Unlike Sherwood, it was not a royal hunting forest and the 'greenwood' aspects of the Robin Hood legend do not feature in the episodes set there. Generally speaking, however, the term refers to an area between Pontefract and Doncaster, defined by the River Aire at Ferrybridge to the north and the Doncaster-Wakefield Road to the south. It is bisected west-east by the River Went and north-south by the Great North Road. This highway originated with the Romans and its route has remained one of England's primary cross-country thoroughfares – today the A1 substantially follows its former course.

In the 'Gest' the Great North Road is referred to by the colloquial term 'Watling Street', and Robin and his men are described waylaying travellers upon it. Reference is also made to their lookout at 'Saylis', which has been identified by Professors Dobson and Taylor as a spot named Sayles Plantation on seventeenth-century maps of the area. This wooded hilltop overlooks a steep valley where the Great North Road once crossed the River Went, and it would undoubtedly have been a favourable position for outlaws to operate from. The place at which the road crosses the river has since developed into the town of Wentbridge, where today a blue plaque commemorates the legendary outlaw's association with the area.

One of the most substantial episodes of the 'Gest' moves from this base at Barnsdale to the city of York, and exemplifies many of the principle themes of the early ballads. After intercepting a knight on the Great North Road and inviting him to eat with them, the outlaws demand to know how much money he is carrying. The knight says only ten shillings and a search by Little John confirms this. Robin inquires how his penury came about and the knight explains that his son killed two men, forcing him to spend all of his money and mortgage his land to St Mary's Abbey in York, in order to save his boy from the gallows.

At hearing of such injustice, Robin loans the knight the £400 he needs to recover his land and sends Little John to York with him. Upon reaching St Mary's, the knight feigns that he does not have the funds and begs the abbot's mercy. The abbot refuses, at which the knight reveals his ruse and pays the abbot, with the admonishment that had the priest been more lenient, he would have been further rewarded. After the knight obtains money with which to repay Robin, he is delayed on his journey by his effort to save a yeoman who is in danger of being harmed by an angry crowd.

Meanwhile, back in Barnsdale, Robin has waylaid a monk from St Mary's and again demands to know how much his guest is carrying. The monk, however, lies and claims that he only has twenty marks, when he actually has £800. Robin discovers his deception and claims it all, declaring that as he had not yet been repaid by the knight, St Mary's owed him the £400 he had lent and must have courteously doubled it! The dishonest monk is sent on his way penniless, and when the knight finally arrives to repay Robin, the outlaw refuses to take it on the grounds that anybody who helps a yeoman is a friend.

This narrative amply illustrates the ballads' animosity towards the wealth and corruption of the Church, represented by the merciless abbot and the dishonest monk. Moreover, it portrays Robin as a fundamentally honest thief. It is implied that had the monk only told the truth about the amount of money he was carrying, the outlaws would not have seized it. Meanwhile, Robin not only refuses to steal from the honest knight but offers to lend him assistance. He later declines the knight's attempts to repay him when his band no longer need the money, on grounds that reinforce the ballads' affinity with the emergent yeoman class. Doubtless these were all sentiments which a late medieval audience would have lapped up, contributing greatly to the ballads' popularity.

Another prevalent feature of the earlier ballads is the combat narrative and in a period when quarterstaff contests were a favourite local pastime, whilst archery practice was compulsory for all men between the ages of fifteen and sixty, these aspects were also a noteworthy factor in the legend's wide appeal. Perhaps most common are the 'Robin meets his match' tales, in which a local character is shown equalling Robin's skill and is subsequently asked to join the outlaws' band. These stories seem to have been designed to flatter regional pride, conveying the message that the named locality is special because it produced an opponent capable of giving Robin Hood, one of the most skilled combatants who ever lived, a run for his money.

Two notable examples of such ballads take place in Yorkshire. The first is 'The Jolly Pinder of Wakefield', the earliest reference to which occur in the Stationers' Register for 1557-9. A pinder is an obsolete medieval profession, an officer of the lord of the manor charged with looking after the town pinfold: an enclosure in which animals that had strayed onto common land were held until they were recovered by their owners, upon the payment of a fine. It was a position of petty authority but at the start of the ballad, the eponymous 'jolly pinder' boasts that such was his power, not even a baron would dare to trespass at Wakefield.

Robin, Little John and Will Scarlett overhear his remark, and determine to take the pinder down a notch and confront him. The pinder asks them to leave the common and return to the highway, but when they refuse, a melee ensues. Despite being outnumbered three-to-one, the pinder is true to his word and proves a match for the outlaws, who are so impressed by his skill in combat, that they ask him to join them. The pinder offers them some food and replies that he will wait until Michaelmas when his wage from the lord of the manor is due, and then proceed to join them in the greenwood.

The second example is 'Robin Hood and the Curtal Friar' which takes place in the vicinity of Fountains Abbey, a Cistercian monastery founded in 1132, near Ripon in North Yorkshire. The earliest surviving version of the ballad is a garland from 1663, although similarities to the play fragment from 1475 suggest that it may have circulated for some considerable time before that printing. A medieval origin is also suggested by the involvement of the friar, as this order of Christian mendicants was abolished in England during the Protestant Reformation. Some later sources have identified the friar in this tale with Friar Tuck, although the name is never used in the original ballad.

In the ballad, Robin speculates that there is no match for Little John within 100 miles, to which Will Scarlett replies that there is rumour of a friar near Fountains Abbey who could best him. Robin finds the friar beside the River Skell and, pretending to be a weary traveller, asks to be carried across the water. The friar agrees, but halfway across throws the outlaw from his back and challenges him to a duel. The two fight with swords for a considerable time until an exhausted Robin begs a favour: to let him blow his horn. The friar assents and Robin uses the horn to summon his men, who appear on the bank with their bows. The friar then begs a favour from Robin: to let him whistle. Robin agrees and the Friar summons a pack of hunting-dogs. Admitting that he is well-matched, Robin refuses to fight further and asks the friar to join his band.

Whilst both 'The Jolly Pinder of Wakefield' and 'The Curtal Friar' represent typical examples of the early ballads' milieu, Yorkshire is also the scene for two of the most unique episodes in the canon. The ballad known as 'Robin Hood's Fishing' (or 'Robin Hood's Preferment') is the only narrative with a nautical theme and despite this departure from the familiar environment, it was seemingly one of the most popular ballads during the seventeenth century, circulating widely in broadside and garland form. It is possibly a late invention, with the coastal setting suggesting that the legend had spread far from its original territory by the time of the ballad's composition. Certainly, no references or analogues exist before an entry in the Stationers' Register for 1631.

'Robin Hood's Fishing' sees the hero grow weary of life in the greenwood and retire to Scarborough, on the North Yorkshire coast, where he takes work as a fisherman. Unsurprisingly, life as an outlaw has not prepared him for such a trade and he is mocked by the crew, who deny him a share of their catch. After several days at sea, the fishing boat is pursued by a French warship; the crew fear they will be captured and taken to France as prisoners, but Robin takes up his bow and picks off most of the French sailors, before boarding the ship with his sword to finish the job. There he discovers £12,000 in gold, which he offers to split with the fishermen. They refuse on the grounds that Robin won it himself, at which he vows to use the spoils to found a haven for the dispossessed.

Although 'Robin Hood's Fishing' might be atypical in its setting, stylistically and thematically it is consistent with many other ballads. The tone is knock-about picaresque and the narrative concludes with a familiar display of Robin's graciousness and largesse. Far more unusual is the account of Robin's death, one of the most momentous episodes in the canon and tonally quite unlike any other ballad. A fatalistic atmosphere pervades the narrative and it closes on a downbeat note – it is the only episode to end in Robin's defeat, and a terminal one at that. Whilst many of the earliest tales of Robin Hood were comedies, without consequences or connection to any wider context, the narrative of the outlaw's death brings a stark and tragic nemesis.

There are two principle sources for the death narrative. The first is the final segment of the 'Gest', but whilst this can be securely dated to the late fifteenth century, the account is synoptic and lacks much in the way of detail or motivation. A fuller account is found in the ballad 'Robin Hood's Death', which regrettably only exists in a damaged fragment of indeterminate date. This manuscript was discovered by Bishop Percy in the 1760s, and dates from the mid-seventeenth century. However, there is internal evidence to suggest that the ballad itself was composed much earlier, probably in the late Middle Ages, and may have been the original source for the truncated version of the narrative which appears in the 'Gest'.

In 'Robin Hood's Death', after living many years as an outlaw, an elderly Robin falls ill and announces his intention to travel to Kirklees Priory, near Huddersfield, to have his blood let – a common medieval cure for a variety of maladies. Will Scarlett warns him against the journey, reminding him that he must travel close

Robin Hood's Grave at Kirklees. (John Billingsley)

to the home of the antagonistic Roger of Doncaster, to which Robin replies that he has nothing to fear, as the prioress is his cousin and would never allow harm to come to him. Nonetheless, he is persuaded to take Little John along with him, but as the two proceed, the foreshadowing grows darker when they encounter an old woman at the crossing of a river, who curses Robin's name.

Upon their arrival at Kirklees, Robin sends Little John to wait for him nearby and allows the prioress to lead him to an upstairs room and open his vein. However, true to Will Scarlett's warning, treachery is afoot. Robin's faithless cousin locks him in the chamber and leaves him to bleed out, both for the wrong the outlaw has done to the Church and to appease her lover, Roger of Doncaster. After the hero has suffered substantial blood loss, he is confronted by Roger and a fight ensues, but even in his weakened state, Robin proves a formidable opponent and slays the villain with a knife to the throat. The prioress retreats and with the last of his strength, Robin blows his horn to summon Little John.

Robin's faithful companion arrives, breaking down doors in his wake, and begs his master to let him burn the nunnery to the ground. Robin refuses this request, stating that he has never harmed a woman and would not allow harm to come to any now. He merely asks that Little John hear his final confession, and then bury his body beside the highway nearby, with his sword at his head, his arrows by his side and his bow at his feet. In later versions of the ballad, Robin chooses the exact site of his grave by loosing a final arrow from the window of the priory and instructing Little John to inter him where it lands. However, whilst this has become the defining image of the outlaw's demise, it does not appear in the original sources and appears to be a Romantic embellishment of the eighteenth century.

Contrary to popular belief, Kirklees is the only site to have been consistently associated with Robin Hood's death since the Middle Ages. Perhaps more remarkably, a monument purporting to be 'Robin Hood's Grave' still exists on land that once belonged to Kirkless Priory. Some commentators have dismissed this site as a gentrified folly, but whilst the grave was enclosed during the eighteenth century to protect it from vandals and a mock epitaph erected alongside it, the gravestone itself shows evidence of being much older. Furthermore, the earliest independent textual reference to the site dates from 1536 – prior to the dissolution of the priory – whilst supporting references continue throughout the sixteenth century. Although the exact provenance of the monument remains a mystery, its relative antiquity cannot be disputed.

Perhaps unsurprisingly, the grave has attracted further folklore over the years. In the eighteenth century, local navvies believed that chippings from the stone offered protection from toothache – one of the main factors in the grave's regrettable depredation. More eerily, in 1730, the historian Thomas Gent recorded that a local knight had not long ago removed the tombstone to use for a hearth in his great hall. However, each morning he rose to find that it had been 'turned aside' by some mysterious force, compelling him to return it to its proper place. Significantly, it required only half the number of animals to drag it back than it had taken to take it away. Both these traditions are common migratory legends, frequently associated with ancient monuments, from prehistoric megaliths to medieval memorials.

All the preceding stories were taken from ballads, and the advent of the printing press formalised and preserved such oral narratives, which may have extended far back into the Middle Ages. However, as the legend grew in popularity during the sixteenth century, a panoply of apocryphal local traditions began to emerge, the origins of which remain controversial. Some may represent lore as old as the ballads themselves, whilst others were probably later inventions inspired by the circulation of those ballads. As J.C. Holt observes, 'There are two obvious causes of the proliferation … The first was psychological: those who told or listened to the stories tried to add to their realism by transferring the hero's name to familiar places in the immediate locality. The second was commercial: innkeepers and other could attract custom by claiming that "Robin Hood was here".'

One of the most oft-repeated examples of these apocryphal traditions is that Robin was born at Loxley, near Sheffield. The belief was first noted in the early seventeenth century in an anonymously written and undated prose chronicle of the outlaw's life. known as the Sloane Manuscript and by the noted antiquary Roger Dodsworth, writing in 1620. Meanwhile, a land survey of 1637 records the ruins of a house at Little Haggas Croft in which the outlaw was supposed to have been born, and which could be seen until 1884. The Loxley legend further maintains that the young Robin was forced into life as an outlaw after he killed his stepfather with a scythe, whilst they were working land at Loxley Chase Farm. He then spent several years hiding out in a cave on Loxley Edge, before he was forced to flee the area altogether.

Robin Hood's Bay, where the legendary outlaw kept a fishing boat. (Phil Roper)

Another location irrevocably associated with the outlaw – this time by virtue of its name – is the picturesque North Yorkshire fishing village, Robin Hood's Bay. The settlement was first recorded under that title by John Leland in 1536, and two legends account for its nomenclature. One asserts that Robin loosed an arrow from Stoupe Brow and vowed to build a town wherever it landed – perhaps the haven he swore to found in 'Robin Hood's Fishing'. The second version reports that Robin's notoriety grew so great that the king sent a great force of soldiers from London to detain him, forcing the outlaw to take refuge on the moors near Whitby. Whilst in the area, he moored a boat at the inlet where Robin Hood's Bay now stands, so that he could escape to sea if necessary and often took it out fishing to pass his days in hiding.

A related legend claims that during this period, the abbot of Whitby invited Robin and Little John to dine with him at the abbey. Whilst they were enjoying his hospitality, the abbot requested a demonstration of their famed archery skill and so the pair ascended to the roof of the building where they each loosed an arrow in the direction of Hawsker. The arrows fell a mile away near Whitby-Laithes, one at each side of the road and Little John's some 100 feet further than Robin's. The abbot was reputedly so impressed that he erected a stone pillar where each arrow landed to commemorate the feat, and whilst the original pillars are no more, the fields in which the arrows supposedly came to ground are still marked as Robin Hood and Little John Close.

Robin Hood toponyms such as these abound throughout Yorkshire. The earliest recorded example is Robin Hood's Stone, mentioned in a cartulary of Monk

Bretton Priory, dated 1422. The exact location of the stone has been lost, but it was appropriately somewhere in Barnsdale. Some scholars have suggested it was close to the site of Robin Hood's Well, which sat beside the Great North Road a short distance south-east of Barnsdale Bar. The well was first recorded by Roger Dodsworth in 1622 and it was the site of a brisk trade for many hundreds of years. Today, however, the spring itself is lost beneath the dual-carriageway of the A1; all that remains is the well house, designed by the illustrious Sir John Vanbrugh *c.* 1720, and now relocated to the side of the road.

Another Robin Hood's Well could once be found on Stanbury Moor near Haworth, accompanied by Little John's Well and Will Scarlett's Well nearby. Although they were practically lost by the time their tradition was recorded in 1899, local legend claimed that the outlaws once drank from these springs. Indeed, if such lore is to be believed, Robin and his men spent a lot of time in this tract of West Yorkshire. Not far away at Rivock Edge, above Keighley, there is a vast boulder known as Robin Hood's Stone beneath which he supposedly slept, whilst similar stories are told of an earthfast boulder known as Robin Hood's Chair and a natural rock-shelter called Robin Hood's House, both at Baildon.

Robin's name seems to have attached itself to a number of monoliths in Yorkshire, both natural and man-made. In some cases, he merely visited the feature but in others, he is responsible for its very existence in the landscape. As the Halifax historian, Reverend John Watson, noted in 1775, 'The country people here attribute everything of the marvellous kind to Robin Hood.' In these stories, Robin takes on the characteristics of a giant – as if his stature has grown to match the magnitude of his deeds – and doubtless his name was transposed over much older legends concerning the deeds of giants, whose titles are now long forgotten. It is a role adopted by King Arthur in other counties across Britain, but in Yorkshire it belongs exclusively to Robin.

Robin Hood's Penny Stone at Wainstalls near Halifax was one such example. This large natural boulder topped by a rocking stone was broken up for building material in the nineteenth century, but prior to that locals claimed Robin Hood once 'used this stone to pitch with at a mark for his amusement.' There is another boulder known as Robin Hood's Penny Stone just over a mile away on Midgley Moor which still survives today. Meanwhile, on the opposite side of the Calder Valley, there was once a standing stone known as Sowerby Lad which Robin was supposed 'to have thrown … off an adjoining hill with a spade as he was digging.' Sadly, this stone has also been destroyed.

A little further away atop Blackstone Edge, on the very border of Yorkshire with Lancashire, there is a rock formation called Robin Hood's Bed. The outlaw is supposed to have slept here and used it as a lookout to observe movement on the ancient highway below. In his gigantic guise, he took one of the many boulders strewn about that place and flung it across the border, where it came to rest 6 miles away on Monstone Edge, and acquired the name Robin Hood's Quoit. The Quoit

Robin Hood's Pennystone on Midgley Moor, hurled by the legendary outlaw? (Kai Roberts)

was in fact a prehistoric burial cairn, and this connection between the outlaw and megaliths is another common theme. A row of tumuli dubbed 'Robin Hood's Butts' near Robin Hood's Bay were supposedly set up by the outlaw for target practice, and the story of the arrows fired from Whitby Abbey may have been a back-formation to account for the names of two ancient standing stones.

Traditions such as these illustrate the difficulties with a purely historical conception of Robin Hood. Although many of his legends take place in a more recognisably historical milieu than those of King Arthur, Robin represents a similarly mythic figure in that the narratives associated with him primarily express the worldviews of communities across time and space, the character acting as a concept onto which humans project their dominant concerns. As a result, to some he is an outlaw, whilst to others he is a giant. What is certain is that he will never be a single, identifiable figure and nor should we wish him to be. Like so many folkloric entities mentioned in this book, he is fundamentally liminal and ambiguous; a shape-shifting trickster who will forever re-emerge in different guises according to the needs of those who imagine him.

THIRTEEN

CALENDAR CUSTOMS
AND THE RITUAL YEAR

In the popular imagination, calendar customs are regarded as one of the most characteristic manifestations of 'folklore' in the modern world. Traditions such as Morris dancing are perceived as an archetypal expression of Britain's enduring folk heritage; an almost immemorial practice which represents the last lingering influence of a distant and idealised past. Yet such a perspective fails to appreciate the malleable and dynamic nature of such customs. They are not rigid inheritances from a previous age and whilst some continuity with earlier generations inheres, they often say as much about the contemporary context in which they are performed as any historical era. Traditions die, and others are created with surprising regularity, whilst those that persist are constantly reinvented to reflect changing demographics and new cultural ideologies.

Research over the last fifty years has increasingly demonstrated that many customs that have long been labelled as the product of remote antiquity, are not nearly as old as we would like to believe. Indeed, anything much older than a couple of generations seems to have acquired the reputation of a timeless, immutable tradition. In some cases, they are barely more than a couple of hundred years old and were not the spontaneous creation of the masses, but a corruption of practices which originated with prevailing hegemonies and expressed the dominant status quo of their age. Similarly, many such customs have been constantly revised over their lifetimes, and have usually undergone extinction and revival several times, especially as a result of major upheavals such as the Reformation, the Commonwealth and the two world wars.

Much of the confusion surrounding calendar customs stems from Victorian models of folklore and anthropology, especially a combination of the 'myth-ritual' and 'survivals' theory, which held that such traditions were relics of pagan rituals designed to ensure the fertility of the land. Morris dancing was regularly interpreted in such terms, although we now know it probably originated as a courtly fashion during the late Middle Ages and was only widely adopted by the general populace in the sixteenth century. Today, calendar customs are understood as having infinitely more diverse origins and functions, including celebrations to mark major points in the agricultural calendar, legitimised forms of begging and half-remembered imitations of forbidden Catholic feasts. This chapter will endeavour to do justice to their multiplicity.

Spring

As soon as the midnight chimes had ushered in 1 January, the ritual year in Yorkshire commenced with a classic 'visiting custom' known as first-footing. This widespread superstition dictated that the first person to cross the threshold of a house in the New Year had to possess certain physical characteristics and perform certain actions, to ensure the luck of the family in the coming year. Conversely, should the first person to cross the threshold possess certain undesirable attributes, then ill-fortune was sure to follow. The stipulations varied wildly from place to place, without any obvious pattern, but as Ronald Hutton observes, typically they 'reinforce prevailing stereotypes of gender dominance and biological normality'.

For instance, in East Yorkshire, the first-footer had to be dark-haired, whilst around the North York Moors they were supposed to be fair. In Skipton, it was considered profoundly unlucky for a red-haired man to be the first to enter a house – to the extent that one family abandoned their home after this had occurred – but only a short distance away in the vicinity of the West Riding towns of Huddersfield and Bradford, red hair was considered the most auspicious attribute. The only commonality in all these places was that the first-footer had to be male. Often they were expected to symbolically brush away the old year, or to bring a spring of holly and lump of coal to place on the hearth. Equally, they were required to enter through the front door only and leave by the back.

As it was typical for first-footers to be rewarded with a donation of victuals or money, it was common for poorer locals who conformed to the specified characteristics to go from house to house offering their services, and like so many visiting customs discussed in this chapter, the practice became a legitimised form of begging in many communities. However, as belief in the efficacy of first-footing waned through the nineteenth century, in some areas those determined to maintain their profits from the tradition turned to coercion. Writing in 1901, a native of Elland in West Yorkshire recalls that during her childhood, 'Unless we kept our doors locked, our houses were invaded by troops of mummers who ... came to sweep the old year out.'

A more unique begging custom took place on New Year's Day morning, in the East Yorkshire market town of Driffield, when children would walk the streets chanting,

> Here we are at our town's end
> A bottle of rum and a crown to spend
> Are we downhearted? No!
> Shall we win? Yes!

At this summons, shopkeepers would come to their door and throw a handful of pennies into the street for which the children would then madly scramble. Until recently, the tradition was entirely unsponsored and spontaneous, but due to its decline during the 1990s, the town council stepped in and now organise it as an official town event.

In agricultural communities, the ritual year was greatly determined by the annual cycles of food production, and so the first farming day of the New Year was marked accordingly. Thus on Plough Monday – the first Monday after Twelfth Night – around the North York Moors and Holderness, teams of farm labourers would process around the parishes dragging a plough and soliciting donations. The Plough Stotts, as they were known, typically dressed with their shirts over their jackets, sashes across their breasts and ribbons on their hats, and were accompanied by a variety of mummers and musicians. As the pageantry grew more elaborate, it ensured that the processions endured long after their original function was obsolete.

In East Yorkshire, the team was accompanied by two disreputable characters; a molly dancer called Besom Bet and Blether Dick, who wore a coat covered in motley rags and carried a bladder attached to the end of a stick, with which he would whack the Plough Stotts as they performed a lewd dance. Meanwhile, in North Yorkshire, the mummers were known as 'Madgies' who cavorted with blackened faces and horned headdresses. The Plough Stotts of some North Yorkshire communities also processed with long-sword dancers, who performed an elaborate routine involving the interlocking of swords, culminating in the symbolic beheading and resurrection of their leader. This tradition continues on Plough Monday in Goathland, following a revival in 1923.

The 20 January marked the Eve of St Agnes, familiar to many from John Keats' classic poem of that name and known in Yorkshire as a time ripe for divinatory practices. Typically, if they performed certain rituals, girls were supposed to receive a vision of the man they would marry. In one example, two girls must fast and remain silent throughout the day, then in the evening bake a mixture of flour, salt and water known as a 'dumb cake'. Once cooked, this must be divided equally into two, and each girl had to carry her piece backwards up the stairs and into her bed, before it could be eaten. If these conditions were fulfilled, the girl was promised her future husband would appear to her in that night's dream.

Kirkburton Rapier Dancers performing at Beverley. (John Billinglsey)

Shrovetide was observed in Yorkshire, as in most places across England, with the consumption of all those rich, perishable foodstuffs which would shortly be forbidden during the Lenten fast – cuts of meat on Collop Monday and pancakes on Shrove Tuesday. But whilst abstinence was observed for forty days and nights from Ash Wednesday, settlements along the Yorkshire coast marked the fifth Sunday of Lent with a feast of sorts. Known as Carlin Sunday, typically unappetising brown peas were fried in pig fat and seasoned with pepper to become 'carlins', whereupon they were consumed with great gusto.

Filey folklore claims the custom began when a ship called *The Carlin* was wrecked near the Brigg, and its cargo of peas washed up on shore. However, as Carlin Sunday is known across much of the north-east coast, it seems unlikely that its origin was so localised. The tradition more probably arose simply because peas were a readily available foodstuff permitted during the fast, and commonly donated in large quantities to the poor during this period by the local gentry. Inevitably, as the practice of fasting during Lent has declined with secularisation, so has the need for Carlin Sunday. Unlike Shrove Tuesday, however, its traditions have been long forgotten.

Lent came to an end with Palm Sunday, traditionally known as a day for gluttony and debauchery across the country. But in certain communities in West Yorkshire, particularly those around Calderdale, a more innocent custom prevailed. On the morning of Palm Sunday, young men and women would take bottles to collect water from the local holy well, which they would then mix with Spanish liquorice to create a concoction known as 'Popolloli'. The gathering was a popular opportunity for courting, and would-be couples could 'plight their troth' by drinking from each other's bottle. The custom was observed until the early twentieth century, but with many old wells falling into disuse, running dry and being built over, it has entirely died out.

Calderdale can boast another distinctive Easter custom known as the 'Pace Egg Play', performed on Good Friday. Like many mummers plays, it is a 'hero-combat drama' in which the protagonist must fight a series of duels, during the last of which he is fatally wounded and then subsequently resurrected. Here the hero is St George, who overcomes villains called the Black Prince of Paradine and Hector, before he is killed by the Bold Slasher and revived by the doctor. Whilst the action unfolds, a fool character named Toss Pot provides a running commentary and capers around the audience. At the end, the Pace Egg Song is sung by the cast, whilst Toss Pot collects donations, suggesting it originated as another example of a legitimised begging.

Whilst the Pace Egg was also performed in certain Lancashire towns, the Calderdale version is unique to the valley. The lyrics to the Pace Egg Song are not replicated elsewhere and the Calderdale mummers are known for their elaborate headgear, which is often worked on for weeks in advance. The play has been presented in the region almost continually for several centuries, and whilst textual references do not exist until the early 1700s, they suggest it was already a thriving tradition. Although performances briefly died out following the Great War, it was revived in 1932 and is continued today by two teams from the hilltop villages of Heptonstall and Midgley – the latter comprised of pupils from Calder High School.

The Pace Egg Play. (Brighouse Children's Theatre)

On Easter Sunday, the rising sun was credited with unusual properties, including the belief that it danced with joy in celebration of the resurrection of Jesus Christ. Known across Europe, the superstition was widely observed in Yorkshire until quite recently, and folk would often ascend a local hill before dawn to witness the spectacle. Beamsley Beacon, above Ilkley, was a particularly favoured location for such gatherings. In the North and East Ridings, a divinatory custom called 'wading the sun' was also practiced, whereby a bucket of water was placed to catch the rising orb. If the sun 'waded' (i.e. was reflected in the water causing it to glimmer) then it promised a fine season to follow.

Easter Monday was marked across the county by egg-rolling games for children, and 'Troll-Egg Day' was a common colloquial name for the festival. But whilst this harmless activity is often revived today, the less savoury tradition of 'buckle-snatching' or 'Leggin' Day' (as it was called in the East Riding) has been consigned to history. Recorded in towns such as Whitby, it was customary for boys to trip girls up and remove their shoes, which they would only return upon payment of some gratuity. Unsurprisingly, this antisocial, uncouth practice sometimes led to riots and like many loutish institutions of a similar ilk, it was stamped out by the establishment of local constabularies in the nineteenth century.

All Fools' Day was on 1 April as it is today; pranks were played on the gullible until noon. Sending some callow youth on a fool's errand was a particularly popular manifestation of this custom; for instance, to collect a pennyworth of pigeon's milk from the chemist or a volume called *The Life of Adam's Father* from a bookseller. A favourite in East Yorkshire was to send a boy to the cobbler's for 'stirrup oil', a request which would be met by a beating from the shoemaker's stirrup. The unlucky dupes were dubbed 'gawks' – a northern dialect word for cuckoo – and the hoaxes were known as 'hunting the gawk'.

The arrival of the cuckoo was a cause for great celebration, as it heralded the onset of summer. In South Yorkshire, a tradition called 'footing the cuckoo' was observed, whereby the first person to hear a cuckoo in the neighbourhood would gather his friends and as many beer barrels as they could carry, take them to the trees in which the bird was heard and proceed to carouse the rest of the day away. It is said that in the Ribblesdale village of Austwick, the locals were so keen to keep the cuckoo and hopefully the summer with it, that they tried to wall it in. The bird simply flew away over the top, but the villagers maintained that 'if they had only built the wall one round of stones higher, the bird could never have got out.' The same tale is told about the West Yorkshire village of Marsden, who celebrate an annual fête called 'Cuckoo Day' in late April.

St Mark's Eve fell on 24 April, and until rationality prevailed in the late nineteenth century, it was another favourite night for divinatory customs. Readings were taken from impressions created by sifting the ash in the hearth (ash-riddling) or the chaff on the barn floor (chaff-riddling). It was also the designated night for a particularly macabre custom known as 'porch-watching'. Across Yorkshire, especially in rural areas, people believed that if an individual kept nocturnal watch in the church porch on St Mark's Eve for three years in a row, on the third vigil they would witness the wraiths of all those who were to die in the parish during the following year process down the corpse road and into the church.

There were many attendant superstitions which varied from place to place, including the belief that anybody who fell asleep whilst porch-watching would themselves die, and that whoever watches the porch once must do so for their whole lifetime. The tradition was a source of dread to many and it was widely exploited by the unscrupulous. A woman named Old Peg Doo used to watch the porch of the Priory Church at Bridlington every year, and charge her neighbours to reveal what she had witnessed. Although veteran porch-watchers were often shunned by the community, it was very easy for them to use their position for malicious ends. It was rumoured that for some people who heard that their wraith had been seen entering the church on St Mark's Eve, it became a self-fulfilling prophecy as they were driven into such a state of anxiety that their death soon followed.

The last day of April, 'May Eve', was marked in Yorkshire as one of the first two 'Mischief Nights' of the year, a time of misrule during which gangs of youths would play a variety of pranks on their unfortunate neighbours, under the illusion the date gave them protection from the law. Typical mischief included everything from simple tricks, such as leading animals astray, securing doors from the outside and removing gates from their hinges, to more elaborate schemes like suspending a needle next to a window to create a persistent and elusive tapping sound, or boarding up the windows to cause the residents to oversleep. As one commentator remarked, 'The first of April is the Fool's day and the last day of that month is the Devil's.'

Summer

May Day itself was widely celebrated in England during the fifteenth and sixteenth centuries, and whilst it was banned during the Commonwealth, festivities were resurrected for a period following the Restoration and again in corrupted form during the nineteenth century, according to the Victorian fashion for a romanticised 'Merrie England'. In its original form, the day was known as a riotous occasion and involved a variety of universal customs, such as maypole dancing and 'bringing in the May', which would see young folk go out into the surrounding countryside to collect foliage with which to decorate the village.

May Day festivities were particularly despised by Puritan reformers during the seventeenth century, who regarded such practices as both pagan and licentious. The nonconformist firebrand and inveterate diarist, Reverend Oliver Heywood, records that around 1630, the vicar of Halifax preached virulently against May Day customs and even attempted to prevent the erection of a maypole, leading to great unrest in the town. Of course, the celebration was thoroughly stamped out by the Commonwealth and whilst a revival followed the Restoration, the traditions gradually changed in form, so that by the nineteenth century, 'bringing in the May' had evolved into more innocent practices such as garlanding, a children's visiting custom. In Yorkshire, a little of the old lustiness endured and young men traditionally left foliage on the doorsteps of any girl they wished to flatter.

One of the most archetypal motifs associated with May Day is the maypole, a central feature of both the early festivities and the Victorian revival. During the nineteenth century, it was so significant that a number of villages in Yorkshire had a permanent maypole – only two survive in the county, but inevitably May Day celebrations remain vibrant in these places. Gawthorpe, near Wakefield, is one such example and their annual pageant features a horseback procession, which parades to the neighbouring town of Ossett and back before the May Queen is crowned beneath the maypole. The current pole is a former pylon donated by Yorkshire Electricity Board and winched into place by crane in 1986.

However, the more famous maypole at Barwick-in-Elmet, near Leeds, is replaced every three years by traditional methods – ladders, rope and human labour. The raising ceremony originally took place on Whit Tuesday, but has now been fixed to Spring Bank Holiday and the event has become more significant than May Day itself. By custom, work begins at 6 p.m. and takes over 100 people at least three hours to complete, during which their exertions are accompanied by a band parade and Morris dancing. Once the maypole is in place, four garlands are hung halfway up and a weather vane in the shape of a fox is fixed to the top. It is said that anybody who is struck by the pole during its erection will be left simple-minded for the

remainder of their days, and the phrase 'knocked at Barwick' was once a local idiom for those considered 'backwards'.

Whilst the sanitised post-Restoration May Day celebrations lost their reputation for public disorder, still some unruliness remained and maypole theft became a common manifestation of rivalry between neighbouring communities. The Barwick maypole was removed twice, first by Garforth in 1829 and again by Aberford in 1907, whilst the Gawthorpe pole was stolen by Chickenley in 1850 and not replaced until 1875. A local, undated narrative from Wharfedale records that when the Burnsall maypole was purloined by a team of cobblers from Thorpe, a team of villagers were sent to retrieve it and a fight broke out; a similar

The maypole at Barwick-in-Elmet.
(Kai Roberts)

The White Rock above Luddenden Dene, repainted ever May Day morn. (Kai Roberts)

confrontation is recorded between the young men of Brighouse and Rastrick in West Yorkshire, around 1785.

Another particularly curious May Day custom still endures in Calderdale, with no precedent elsewhere in England. First recorded in 1890, a rock on the hillside above the Cat i' th' Well pub, between the villages of Saltonstall and Wainstalls, is painted white every May Day morning. Nobody seems to know who performs the duty or why it originated, although a number of local tales surround the custom. In some narratives, it marks the location of buried treasure, whilst in others it is painted by the Devil himself. However, the proximity of St Catherine's Well at Saltonstall (which gave its name in a corrupted form to the nearby pub) suggests it may originally have been connected with Spaw Sunday (*See* Chapter Ten).

The Feast of the Ascension took place forty days after Easter Sunday and whilst this was primarily a liturgical observance, the preceding three days were known as 'Rogationtide'. During this period, a tradition called 'Beating the Bounds' was performed, whereby the boundaries of the parish were perambulated by civic and ecclesiastic officials alongside local residents. In the days before accurate cartography, the purpose of this custom was to fix these borders in the minds of the populace and thereby reduce the risk of future disputes. Although the function was primarily an administrative one, it had become entangled with an earlier religious procession which had once taken place on the Feast of the Ascension, and so the clergy remained actively involved in the tradition, often preaching a sermon at significant landmarks.

Young boys were also taken on these perambulations, and a variety of techniques were employed to ensure they accurately preserved the knowledge for future generations. In some parishes such as Beverley, the carrot was preferred over the stick, and money, nuts and oranges were thrown out at points which needed committing to memory. At Whitby, laces, pins and biscuits were distributed, whilst one point along the boundary was marked by the Battering Stone – a large mass of whinstone which the boys would pelt with rocks. Any boy who chipped the stone would be rewarded with a guinea from the parish coffers. There was a boundary marker at Flaxton, in Ryedale, known as the Rambleations Stone, from the top of which bread was thrown into the crowd. However, after this custom resulted in riots on several occasions, the practice was discontinued and the stone destroyed.

Some parishes preferred more austere methods of guaranteeing the boys retained a memory of the boundaries. In the Forest of Galtres, boys were 'bumped' at regular stations, whilst in other places they were thrown in a ditch or even whipped. In the city of York, this practice was inverted and local boys would whip the parish clerk with bundles of sedge as he stopped to record details. Also perhaps the most bizarre convention associated with 'Beating the Bounds' took place near York, at Water Fulford. Here, at one station along the route, a chicken was set loose and chased by the boys. Whoever caught the bird was rewarded with five shillings, whilst the poor chicken was decapitated and its severed head placed on top of a post marking the boundary!

The practice of Beating the Bounds mostly died out once its civic and legal function was no longer necessary, although its spirit is preserved in the parish boundary walks which take place in some areas at Whitsun. A Rogationtide tradition which still endures, however, is the Whitby Penny Hedge. The hedge is constructed on the shore of the town at 9 a.m. on Ascension Eve, after which a horn is blown to mark that the obligation is complete. The hedge is woven from sticks of hazel and willow, using only a knife of 'a penny price', and it must be strong enough to withstand three tides.

A local legend claims that the tradition started during the twelfth century, when several men murdered a hermit who had given shelter to a boar they were hunting. It is said that the hermit gave instructions for the erection of the Penny Hedge with his dying breath, to be undertaken as a penance to atone for their sin. However, there is no evidence to support this narrative and the ritual actually seems to be a remembrance of an early medieval land-tenure custom, whereby tenants of Whitby Abbey were expected to maintain something called the 'Horngarth' or else their lands would be forfeit. The precise purpose of the Horngarth has been forgotten, although the name suggests it was probably an enclosure for the abbey's cattle.

As in all counties of England, Whitsuntide in Yorkshire was a time for fairs and feasting as the climate had warmed sufficiently by this time to allow outdoor gatherings. In the fifteenth and sixteenth century, Whitsun was the traditional occasion for the May Games, which the Victorians later incorporated into their revived May Day celebrations. These typically involved the election of a King and Queen of Summer, Robin Hood plays, feats of sportsmanship and morris dancing. In later centuries, the more unique custom of 'Chalk Back Neet' was recorded around Bridlington, when local boys and girls would gather on the church green armed with a stick of chalk and attempt to mark each others' backs.

Royal Oak, or Oak Apple, Day was celebrated on 29 May from 1661, to commemorate the Restoration of Charles II to the throne following the Commonwealth. Whilst most Royal Oak Day traditions in Yorkshire seem to have died out by the mid-twentieth century, it was once tradition to deck public buildings with oak and for men to wear oaken twigs in their caps. Anybody who did not display such an adornment was pelted with rotten eggs or rubbed with nettles. In some villages, such as Great Ayrton in North Yorkshire, it was also customary for children to lock their teacher out of the school, whilst they chanted:

It's Royal Oak Day
It's the 29th of May
If you don't give us a holiday
We'll all run away!

Midsummer fires – which many scholars now regard as one of the few truly pre-Christian survivals in the ritual year – were recorded on the eve of the summer solstice in both North and East Yorkshire as late as the nineteenth century. Traditionally, the bones of dead animals were burnt (known as a 'bone-fire', from which some authorities believe the word 'bonfire' is derived) and spectators were expected to leap through the flames. The superstitious supposed this ritual to purify the community, along with their crops and livestock, protecting them from the various diseases and blights which were more virulent during the hot summer months.

Village feasts took place throughout the summer and were regarded as a highlight of the village calendar. The date of these festivities was usually determined by the feast of the saint to whom the local parish church was dedicated, and often lasted for several days. For instance, the annual celebrations at Halifax began on 24 June with the Feast of St John the Baptist (to whom Halifax Minster is dedicated) and continued until 'Thump Sunday' – a name which local etymology claimed came from the tradition of thumping anybody who entered a pub on that day and refused to pay for a round of drinks. This day was also associated with the consumption of a dish called 'Thump Pudding', which resembled Christmas cake.

The feasting weeks were commonly known as 'wakes' and following the Industrial Revolution in the mill towns of West Yorkshire, it became customary for all factories, shops and other businesses to shut down for the duration. Fairs would often set up on a local recreation ground, featuring stalls, games, dances and all manner of other carnival attractions. Unsurprisingly, wakes became notorious for public drunkenness and brawling, provoking great opprobrium from the more respectable members of Victorian society, who regularly attempted to suppress the celebrations. Nonetheless, the wakes were usually popular enough to survive these attacks, and only really came to an end with the decline of the textile industry in the mid-twentieth century.

Settlements which did not have a parish church, or whose patron saint was commemorated during the colder months, often transferred their feasts to Whitsuntide or early September, where they became associated with rush-bearing. But some places selected more locally significant times to celebrate and it is perhaps not surprising that these customs have proved more enduring. At least two are still celebrated today. The Hepworth Feast takes places on the last weekend in June and supposedly remembers the Holme Valley village's deliverance from the Great Plague of 1665. Meanwhile, the Kilburn Feast is held on the first Sunday after 6 July, the former date of the illustrious horse fair. Kilburn's festivities notably feature the election of a mock Lord Mayor and Lady Mayoress – the latter a man in drag – who parade the streets 'fining' onlookers as they proceed.

Perhaps the most unique and sinister custom associated with a village feast is known as the Burning of Bartle, which takes place on the evening of the Saturday following St Bartholemew's Day (24 August) in the Wensleydale village of West Witton. A giant human effigy made from flammable materials known as 'Bartle' is paraded around the streets followed by a crowd of locals, until they reach the far end of the village, where the effigy is symbolically stabbed and then burned, whilst the assembled onlookers cheer enthusiastically. During the procession, the effigy is halted at certain houses and an immemorial verse recited. The lyrics of this doggerel run thus:

> At Penhill Crags, he tore his rags
> At Hunter's Thorn, he blew his horn
> At Capplebank Stee, he brak his knee
> At Grassgill Beck, he brak his kneck
> At Waddam's End, he couldn't fend
> At Grassgill End, he made his end.

Many explanations have been offered to account for this custom. Some commentators have claimed it is a surviving pre-Christian rite, but as the tradition is not recorded until the late nineteenth century, this is both impossible to prove and highly suspect. Others have connected it with the legend of the Penhill Giant (*See* Chapter Four), although the most popular local explanation is that it remembers the pursuit and mob execution of a local pig thief. However, considering both the name of the effigy and the date of the event, it seems more likely to be connected with St Bartholemew himself. During the Middle Ages, it was not unusual for the effigies of saints to be paraded on their feast days; nor was it unusual for such effigies to be conspicuously destroyed as 'popish superstitions' following the Reformation.

Village feasts and wakes were also commonly associated with the tradition of rush-bearing. This practice originated in a time before pews were common in churches and the congregation were expected to endure lengthy sermons whilst sat on the cold stone floor. As a result, during the summer, the local population would gather rushes from the surrounding countryside to strew across the church floor, to provide a modicum of comfort and warmth through the winter months. Over time, the practice grew into such an elaborate and widely enjoyed ritual that it persisted long

Sowerby Bridge rushbearing. (Tania Poole)

after its original function was redundant. Indeed, its popularity was such that it spread to settlements which had never had a parish church in the first place.

The focus of the rush-bearing festivities became the elaborately decorated rush-cart, and rushes were now collected to construct a teetering pyramid on the back of a cart, which would be symbolically processed around the churches of the district, accompanied by morris dancers and much merrymaking. At one time, rush-bearing was known throughout Yorkshire, but declined during the nineteenth century, until Halliwell Sutcliffe, writing in 1899, spoke of Haworth in West Yorkshire as one of the last places in the county to observe the custom. However, rush-bearing was revived in the Calderdale town of Sowerby Bridge in 1977. Originally, it was intended as a one-off event to mark the Queen's Silver Jubilee, but proved such a success that it now takes place annually on the first weekend in September.

Autumn

By the autumn equinox, the harvest had usually been gathered, which for agricultural communities across the county was cause for another celebration – especially in primarily arable areas such as East Yorkshire and the Vale of York. Once the last sheaf of corn had been brought home, weeks of toil culminated in a feast known as the 'Mell Supper'. As both landowners and labourers tended to collaborate during harvesting, the Mell Supper was an unusually egalitarian tradition during which the whole community, from farmhands to country gentlemen, shared a meal together. Afterwards there would be singing and dancing, often accompanied by the mischief of guisers who, with their sinister, painted faces and rowdy behaviour, were not always welcome.

The last sheaf of corn cut was often brought back with great ceremony, mounted on the back of a cart and then positioned to preside over the ensuing feast. Sometimes they were woven into overtly human effigies known as 'Mell Dolls' and whilst this tradition had largely died out by the mid-twentieth century, it has been extensively revived by country crafts enthusiasts. Less well remembered is a Holderness tradition called 'Burning the Witch' whereby dried bundles of peas were set alight in the field where the last sheaf had been cut, whilst labourers caroused around it. The peas were consumed and ash from the fire used to blacken the faces of those in attendance. The name of this custom suggests that it may have started as an apotropaic practice to protect the farm from witchcraft during the coming winter.

On 18 October the Feast of St Luke was celebrated in the liturgical calendar, but in several cities across Yorkshire it was also once known as 'Whip Dog Day'. As the name suggests, it was customary on this day to strike stray dogs and drive them out of town. In York, legend claimed the practice began when a priest performing Mass on St Luke's Day dropped the host and it was gobbled up by a passing dog. The outraged congregation pursued and killed the unfortunate beast, but that was not enough to atone for its sin and dogs were persecuted on St Luke's Day for evermore. The incident is said to have occurred at the now demolished Church of St Crux, and the custom gave its name to Whip-Ma-Whop-Ma Gate nearby, but this is probably mere fancy.

In Hull, however, they tell a different story. There the practice was supposed to have originated when the dog stole a joint of meat, which was traditionally provided by monks to the poor of the city on St Luke's Day. When the assembled masses learnt of this, they hunted down the offending animal and dispatched it. The custom seems to have taken place in a couple of other cities, including Sheffield, although their local explanations are not recorded and such aetiologies notwithstanding, it seems more likely that Whip Dog Day began as a civic expedient to rid cities of stray dogs.

Historically, All Hallows' Eve was not extensively celebrated in its own right in Yorkshire, although it seems to have been regarded as another time at which divinatory practices were particularly effective. In North Yorkshire, for instance, it was known as 'Nut Crocking Neet' and unmarried girls performed love auguries by throwing nuts into a bonfire. If they stayed on the fire and burnt quickly, it prophesised a happy marriage; but if the nut bounced and flew asunder, a miserable union was foretold. Such divinations seem to have entirely died out with the hegemony of the modern Halloween, although the game of apple-bobbing has been suggested as a corrupted remembrance of these rites.

Trick or Treat is now the most common practice associated with the night countrywide and widely derided as an import from America. However, in the north and west of England, a similar children's visiting custom known as soul-caking was always popular around this time of year, albeit on the following night – All Souls' Eve. Typically, poor children would tour the neighbourhood, stopping at each house to recite the rhyme: 'A soul-cake, a soul-cake, have mercy on all Christian souls for a soul-cake.' At this, the householder would be expected to provide them with a piece of parkin before they would go on their way. In later centuries, once the significance of the soul-cake itself had long been forgotten, other gifts were sometimes distributed.

The practice arose from the Catholic belief that the souls of the dead must spend time undergoing purification in Purgatory before being admitted to Heaven, but their stretch there could be shortened by the prayers of the living. All Souls' Day was a set aside in the liturgical calendar to remember the dead, and so, on this day in the Middle Ages, it became customary for the poor to tour their wealthier neighbours begging for food in the form of a 'soul-cake', in return for prayers to speed their deceased relatives through Purgatory. Protestantism had no truck with concepts such as Purgatory or All Souls' Day, but whilst the Reformation swept these ideas away the practice of soul-caking continued in many areas for many centuries afterwards, although its original function was forgotten. The popularity of the children's visiting custom waned during the nineteenth century, although many places still made soul-cakes on this day and it was considered lucky to keep a few uneaten in the house until the following year. However, a small pocket of traditional soul-caking endured around South Yorkshire until the late twentieth century, especially in the villages of Stannington and Dungsworth, where 1 November was known locally as 'Cakin' Neet'. Whilst the children went from house to house with turnip lanterns, adults donned the mantle of guisers and congregated in the Crown & Glove pub where victuals were provided. Sadly, however, even this last remnant of All Souls' Eve seems to have been usurped by Halloween.

Winter

A second Mischief Night was traditionally celebrated on 4 November and still survives in some of the industrial regions of West Yorkshire, although in many cases the whole period between Halloween and Guy Fawkes' Night has now become one long period of misrule. Customs were similar to those practiced on 30 April, although in recent years, the game of knock-a-door-run has become especially favoured, possibly because, in this day and age, some of the more extreme pranks discussed earlier are likely to lead to charges of criminal damage. Considering the nastiness of some of these older traditions, those who today bemoan the depredations of trick or treating should count their blessings.

Christmas traditions in Yorkshire typically began
in the week preceding the festival itself, with
children's visiting customs and mummers
plays – although in some areas these are
recorded starting as early as Martinmas
(11 November). In Beverley, for instance,
performances featuring Besom Bet and
Blether Dick were familiar around this time.
Writing in 1890, John Nicholson notes, 'Often their disguise is so complete that
at lonely houses they are rude and bold, demanding money or drink in such a
way as to terrify the women who have been left at home. The writer has a vivid
recollection of his mother keeping one of these fellows at bay with a sweeping
brush, while he bolted the door to prevent any farther inroad.'

In the run up to Christmas Eve, the gentler custom of wassailing was particularly
widespread amongst children in the county. Groups would proceed from door to
door carrying a box called the 'Vessel Cup', which contained two dolls representing
the Virgin and Child on a bed of crimped paper, silver stars and flowers. Sometimes
they would also carry a holly branch decorated with ribbons, dolls and oranges.
The party would sing a variety of carols and the 'Wassailing Song', the lyrics of
which ran:

Here we come a-wassailing
Among the leaves so green
Here we come a wandering
So fair to be seen.

As with all visiting customs, the householders were expected to offer the children
a small reward for their performance, typically some small change or appropriate
festive fare – indeed, it was considered profoundly unlucky to turn away the first
wassailers of the season.

On Christmas Eve it was also tradition for a family to bring the yule log into
the house, which should be lit from a fragment of the previous year's log. Along
with a yule candle, it was left to burn all night to represent the Star of Bethlehem.
People considered it an ill-omen for the yule log and candle to burn out before the
dawn, and it was similarly unlucky to give out light from the house or sweep the
ashes from the hearth. In some places, the lighting of the yule log was accompanied
by great ceremony. One writer records that the log had first to be laid on the
hearthrug, whilst the family gathered round and each made three wishes. Once it
was set alight, they feasted on gingerbread, cheese, mince pies and a seasonal dish
called 'frummety' (a type of porridge made from creaved wheat and milk, fruited
with raisins). In South Yorkshire, meanwhile, a posset pot was sent around the table
from which each member of the family should drink.

In Dewsbury, the Church of All Saints (now known as Dewsbury Minster) practices a unique bell-ringing custom on Christmas Eve known as 'Tolling the Devil's Knell'. First, a bell known as 'Nine Tellers' is rung in five sets of five. This arrangement is known as a 'passing bell' and was traditionally sounded in rural parishes to indicate the death of somebody in the parish. As the passing bell struck four times for a man and three times for a woman, the number five is supposed to signify the apocryphal belief that Christ's birth represented the death of the Devil. Somewhat contradictorily, the ringing of the passing bell on Christmas Eve is also supposed to protect the town of Dewsbury from the Devil's influence in the coming year.

Following the passing bell, the tenor bell is chimed once for every year since the birth of Christ and timed so that the final strike coincides with midnight. Legend claims that the observance remembers a crime of Sir Thomas de Soothill, a fifteenth-century noble who, in a fit of rage, threw a servant boy into an iron forge or a local dam. As a penance, he provided the tenor bell for the church and initiated the tradition of Tolling the Devil's Knell. However, the truth of this legend is debatable and indeed, the provenance of the custom remains unclear. No references to it exist before the nineteenth century and whilst Reverend John Buckworth is supposed to have 'revived' the practice in 1828, he may have invented it entirely.

In some places, it was common to 'let in Christmas' at dawn; a practice which had much in common with first-footing on New Year's Day. Similar rules about behaviour and appearance governed the ritual: a boy of a certain hair colour should be first across a household's threshold on Christmas morn; he must enter by the front door carrying a sprig of evergreen; then once the family has provided him with a sixpence or some repast, he must leave by the back door. As with first-footing, this became a regular role on Christmas Day for poorer members of the community endowed with the requisite physical characteristics. They were referred to as 'lucky birds' and held in great esteem at that time of year.

Long-sword dancers traditionally performed on Boxing Day in many communities across Yorkshire, and the custom endures today in a small number of places including Flamborough, Grenoside and Handsworth. The Handsworth area of South Yorkshire – along with Norton, Woodhouse and Upperthorpe – was also known during this period for a mummers play called 'T'Owd Tup'. The performance was perhaps more common around neighbouring parishes in Derbyshire and Nottinghamshire, and when S.O. Addy wrote about the tradition in 1901, it was already dying out in the Sheffield region. However, it has clung on in some isolated pockets and been subject to periodic revival throughout the twentieth century.

Like many mummers plays, T'Owd Tup is a hero-combat play, performed door-to-door by a group typically comprised of several lads from the local area. 'Tup' is an archaic term for a ram and one boy is dressed as the eponymous beast, swaddled in sheets of tarpaulin and carrying a head fashioned from wood, with marbles for eyes and a red flannel for a tongue. The narrative of the play would see the Tup led to market, slaughtered by the Butcher, then restored to life by the Doctor, whilst Our Owd Lass and Little Devil Doubt capered around. The performance would climax with a rendition of the well-known folk song, 'The Derby Ram', after which the players would be given donations for their efforts.

A similar custom by the name of the Poor Old Hoss was performed in the North Yorkshire town of Richmond. In this case, the ram became a horse and the other players dressed as huntsmen, forcing it to canter around until the symbolic arrival of winter, when the Hoss lay down to die and was subsequently resurrected. For a time in the mid-twentieth century, the head of the Hoss was an actual horse skull and thoroughly terrified the local children. Performances of the Poor Old Hoss persist today, although rather than tour Richmond's pubs throughout the festive season, the custom is now confined to Christmas Eve in the marketplace and is thoroughly endorsed by the local council.

Some might argue that like too many surviving calendar customs in the county, such mummery has been sanitised and divorced from its original constituency. Where once they were spontaneous expressions arising from the community itself and often strongly disliked by anyone who aspired to respectability, these traditions have been co-opted by the authorities who now present them as a harmless sideshow for the amusement of tourists and aggrandisement of local dignitaries. They have been taken from the folk and their original subversive function has been lost. As such, they exist purely as whimsical historic relics, whilst living folklore has long since moved on and flows unnoticed in a subtle current all around us.

BIBLIOGRAPHY

Addy, Sidney Oldall: *Household Tales with Other Traditional Remains* (1895)

Ahier, Philip: *The Legends and Traditions of Huddersfield and Its District* (1944)

Atkinson, John Christopher: *Forty Years in a Moorland Parish: Reminiscences and Researches in Danby in Cleveland* (1891)

Ibid.: *The Last of the Giant Killers; Or the Exploits of Sir Jack of Danby Dale* (1891)

Ibid.: *Memorials of Old Whitby; Or Historical Gleanings from Ancient Whitby Records* (1894)

Baker, Margaret: *Folklore and Customs of Rural England* (1974)

Baring-Gould, Sabine: *Yorkshire Oddities, Incidents and Strange Events* (1890)

Ibid.: *Strange Survivals: Some Chapter in the History of Man* (1905)

Bennett, Gillian: *Traditions of Belief: Women, Folklore and the Supernatural Today* (1987)

Bennett, Paul: *The Old Stones of Elmet* (2001)

Billingsley, John: *Stony Gaze: Investigating Celtic and Other Stone Heads* (1998)

Ibid.: *Folk Tales from Calderdale Vol. 1* (2007)

Ibid.: *The Mixenden Treasure* (2009)

Ibid.: *Hood, Head and Hag: Further Folk Tales from Calderdale* (2011)

Blakeborough, John Fairfax: *The Hand of Glory and Further Grandfather's Tales and Legends of Highwaymen and Others* (1924)

Blakeborough, Richard: *Wit, Character, Folklore and Customs of the North Riding of Yorkshire* (1898)

Bogg, Edmund: *From Edenvale to the Plains of York: Or A Thousand Miles in the Valleys of the Nidd and Yore* (1894)

Ibid.: *Wensleydale and the Lower Vale of the Yore, from Ouseburn to Lunds Fell* (1899)

Ibid.: *The Old Kingdom of Elmet: The Land 'Twixt Aire and Wharfe* (1902)

Ibid.: *Higher Wharfeland: The Dale of Romance from Ormscliffe to Cam Fell* (1904)

Ibid.: *Lower Wharfeland: The Old City of York and the Ainsty* (1904)

Bord, Janet and Colin: *Sacred Waters: Holy Wells and Water Lore in Britain and Ireland* (1985)

Briggs, Katharine: *The Fairies in Tradition and Literature* (1967)

Campbell, Marie: *Curious Tales of Old West Yorkshire* (1999)

Ibid.: *Strange World of the Brontës* (2001)

Cass, Eddie: *The Pace Egg Plays of the Calder Valley* (2004)

Clarke, David: *Strange South Yorkshire: Myth, Magic and Memory In the Don Valley* (1994)

Ibid.: *A Guide to Britain's Pagan Heritage* (1995)

Ibid.: *The Head Cult: Tradition and Folklore Surrounding the Symbol of the Severed Human Head in the British Isles* (1998)

Clarke, David and Roberts, Andy: *Twilight of the Celtic Gods* (1996)

Clarke, David and Wilson, Rob: *Strange Sheffield: Legends, Folklore and Mysteries of Hallamshire* (1987)

Cobley, Fred: *On Foot through Wharfedale* (1882)

Cudworth, William: *Rambles Round Horton: Historical, Topographical and Descriptive* (1886)

Davies, Owen: *The Haunted: A Social History of Ghosts* (2007)

Dawson, William Harbutt: *A History of Skipton* (1882)

Dixon, John Henry: *Chronicles and Stories of the Craven Dales* (1881)

Dodd, Gerald: *Ghosts and Legends of Brontë Land* (1986)

Dyer, T.F. Thistleton: *Strange Pages from Family Papers* (1895)

Edwards, Gillian: *Hobgoblin and Sweet Puck: Names and Natures of Fairies* (1974)

Gee, H.L.: *Folk Tales of Yorkshire* (1952)

Gomme, George Laurence: *Folk-lore Reclis or Early Village Life* (1883)

Grainge, William: *The Vale of Mowbray: A Historical and Topographical Account of Thirsk and Its Neighbourhood* (1859)

Grinsell, Leslie: *Folklore of Prehistoric Sites in Britain* (1976)

Gutch, Eliza: *Examples of Printed Folk-lore Concerning the North Riding of Yorkshire, York and the Ainsty* (1901)

Ibid.: *Examples of Printed Folk-lore Concerning the East Riding of Yorkshire* (1912)

Harker, Bailey John: *Rambles in Upper Wharfedale* (1869)

Harte, Jeremy: *Explore Fairy Traditions* (2004)

Ibid.: *English Holy Wells: A Sourcebook* (2008)

Hartley, Marie and Ingilby, Joan: *Wensleydale* (1946)

Ibid.: *Life and Tradition in the Yorkshire Dales* (1981)

Hayman, Richard: *Riddles in Stone: Myths, Archaeology and the Ancient Britons* (2006)

Henderson, William: *Notes on the Folk-lore of the Northern Counties of England and the Borders Vol. 2* (1879)

Heywood, Oliver: The Whole Works of the Rev. Oliver Heywood with Memoirs of His Life' (1825)

Hole, Christina: *Haunted England* (1940)

Holt, J.C. *Robin Hood* (1989)

Hope, Robert Charles: *The Legendary Lore of the Holy Wells of England* (1893)

Hunter, Joseph: *History of Hallamshire* (1819)

Hutton, Ronald: *The Pagan Religions of the Ancient British Isles: Their Nature and Legacy* (1993)

Ibid.: *The Triumph of the Moon: A History of Modern Pagan Witchcraft* (1995)

Ibid.: *The Rise and Fall of Merry England: The Ritual Year 1400-1700* (1996)

Ibid.: *Stations of the Sun: A History of the Ritual Year in Britain* (2001)

Ingram, John Henry: *The Haunted Homes and Family Traditions of Great Britain* (1886)

Jackson, Sidney: *Celtic and Other Stone Heads* (1973)

Leyland, John: *The Yorkshire Coast and the Cleveland Hills and Dales* (1892)

Linahan, Liz: *Pit Ghosts, Padfeet and Poltergeists* (1994)

Ibid.: *More Pit Ghosts, Padfeet and Poltergeists* (1996)

Lofthouse, Jessica: *North Country Folklore* (1976)

Lucas, Joseph: *Studies in Nidderdale* (1882)

MacQuoid, Thomas and Katharine: *About Yorkshire* (1894)

Merrifield, Ralph: *The Archaeology of Ritual and Magic* (1988)

Mitchell, W.R.: *Haunted Yorkshire* (1990)

Montagu, Frederic: *Gleaning in Craven: A Tour from Bolton Abbey to Ambleside* (1838)

Morris, Marmaduke Charles Frederick: *Yorkshire Folk Talk* (1892)

Moss, Fletcher: *Folk-lore, Old Customs and Tales of My Neighbours* (1898)

Nicholson, John: *Folk Lore of East Yorkshire* (1890)

Ord, John Walker: *The History and Antiquities of Cleveland* (1846)

Oxley, Cyril Thomas: *Ghost Tales of the North Country* (1950)

Ibid.: *The Haunted North Country* (1973)

Parkinson, Thomas: *Yorkshire Legends and Traditions: As Told by Her Ancient Chroniclers, Her Poets and Journalists Vol. 1* (1888)

Parkinson, Thomas: *Yorkshire Legends and Traditions: As Told by Her Ancient Chroniclers, Her Poets and Journalists Vol. 2* (1889)

Pegg, Bob: *Rites and Riots: Folk Customs of Britain and Europe* (1981)

Pennick, Nigel: *Skulls, Cats and Witch Bottles* (1986)

Phillips, Guy Ragland: *Brigantia: A Mysteriography* (1976)

Phillips, John: *The Rivers, Mountains and Seacoast of Yorkshire* (1853)

Pobjoy, H.N.: *The Story of the Ancient Parish of Hartshead-cum-Clifton* (1972)

Roberts, Andy: *Ghosts and Legends of Yorkshire* (1992)

Roberts, Kai: *Grave Concerns: The Follies and Folklore of Robin Hood's Final Resting Place* (2011)

Robinson, C. Clough: *The Dialect of Leeds and Its Neighbourhood* (1862)

Robinson, Francis Kildale: *A Glossary of Yorkshire Words and Phrases, Collected in Whitby and the Neighourhood* (1855)

Robinson, W.R.: *Guide to Richmond* (1833)

Ross, Frederick: *Legendary Yorkshire* (1892)

Shepherd, Valerie: *Holy Wells In and Around Bradford* (1994)

Ibid.: *Holy Wells of West Yorkshire and the Dales* (2004)

Simpson, Jacqueline: *British Dragons* (1980)

Simpson, Jacqueline and Roud, Steve: *A Dictionary of English Folklore* (2000)

Smith, Julia: *Fairs, Feasts and Frolics: Customs & Traditions in Yorkshire* (1989)

Smith, William & Collyer, Robert: *Old Yorkshire* (1884)

Southwart, Elizabeth: *Brontë Moors and Villages from Thornton to Haworth* (1923)

Speight, Harry: *Through Airedale from Goole to Malham* (1891)

Ibid.: *The Craven and North-West Yorkshire Highlands* (1892)

Ibid.: *Nidderdale and the Garden of the Nidd* (1894)

Ibid.: *Romantic Richmondshire* (1897)

Ibid.: *Chronicles and Stories of Old Bingley* (1899)

Ibid.: *Upper Wharfedale* (1900)

Ibid.: *Lower Wharfedale* (1902)

Ibid.: *Kirkbyoverblow and District* (1903)

Spence, Lewis: *The Minor Traditions of British Mythology* (1948)

Ibid.: British Fairy Origins: The Genesis and Development of Fairy Legends in British Tradition (1946)

Stringfellow, Garry: *Rushes and Ale: A Brief History of Rushbearing* (2010)

Sutcliffe, Halliwell: *By Moor and Fell* (1909)

Ibid.: The Striding Dales (1929)

Thomas, Keith: *Religion and the Decline of Magic* (1971)

Trubshaw, Bob: *Explore Folklore* (2002)

Trubshaw, Bob (Ed.): *Explore Phantom Black Dogs* (2005)

Turner, Joseph Horsfall: *Haworth Past and Present: A History of Haworth, Stanbury and Oxenhope* (1879)

Ibid.: The History of Brighouse, Rastrick and Hipperholme (1893)

Ibid.: Ancient Bingley, Or Bingley, Its History and Scenery (1897)

Walker, Peter: *Folk Tales from the North York Moors* (1990)

Ibid.: Folk Stories from the Yorkshire Dales (1991)

Ibid.: Folk Tales from York and the Wolds (1992)

Walsham, Alexandra: *The Reformation of the Landscape: Religion, Identity and Memory in Early Modern Britain and Ireland* (2011)

Watson, John: *The History and Antiquities of the Parish of Halifax* (1775)

Westwood, Jennifer: *Albion: A Guide to Legendary Britain* (1986)

Whelan, Edna and Taylor, Ian: *Yorkshire Holy Wells and Sacred Springs* (1989)

Whitlock, Ralph: *Here Be Dragons* (1983)

Wilcock, D.T.: *Stories and Folklore from the District Called Hardcastle Crags* (1921)

Newspapers & Periodicals

Bradford Antiquary
Bradford Observer
Dalesman
Halifax Courier and Guardian
Folklore Magazine
Leeds Mercury
Sheffield and Rotherham Independent
Transactions of the Halifax Antiquarian Society
Yorkshire Herald
Yorkshire Folk-lore
Yorkshire Notes and Queries

INDEX

About the Author

Kai Roberts lives in the Calderdale region of Yorkshire and spent his childhood immersed in the curious traditions of the area. He has written a number of books on folklore and local history, and is especially interested in the relationship between landscape and legend.

If you enjoyed this book, you may also be interested in …

Haunted Huddersfield

KAI ROBERTS

Featuring a terrifying range of apparitions, from poltergeists and ghosts to ancient spirits, haunted buildings and historical horrors, *Haunted Huddersfield* is sure to fascinate everyone with an interest in the town's haunted history and is guaranteed to make your blood run cold.

978 0 7524 6790 0

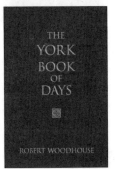

The York Book of Days

ROBERT WOODHOUSE

Taking you through the year day by day, *The York Book of Days* contains amusing, shocking, amazing and important events from different periods in the history of the city. Featuring hundreds of snippets of information and covering the social, criminal, political, religious, agricultural, industrial and sporting history of York, this book will delight residents and visitors alike.

978 0 7524 6045 1

Yorkshire Villains: Rogues, Rascals and Reprobates

MARGARET DRINKALL

Featuring tales of highwaymen, cut throats, poachers, poisoners, thieves and murderers, all factions of the criminal underworld are included in this macabre selection of historic tales. Drawing on a wide variety of sources and containing many cases which have never before been published, *Yorkshire Villains* will fascinate everyone interested in true crime and the history of Yorkshire.

978 0 7524 6002 4

Sheffield: A Pocket Miscellany

JONATHAN SKEWS

From the momentous to the outlandish, this book is packed full of fun facts and trivia about everything Sheffield. From famous quotations and local lingo to the steepest hill and the world's oldest football club, it's all here in this addictive little book.

978 0 7524 6624 8

Visit our website and discover thousands of other History Press books.

www.thehistorypress.co.uk